Ben Pentreath

ENGLISH DECORATION

BIRDS

Ben Pentreath

ENGLISH DECORATION

Timeless Inspiration for the Contemporary Home

with a foreword by Nicky Haslam

photography by Jan Baldwin

LONDON • NEW YORK

To Anthony Sykes, who understands more about English decoration than anyone I know.

SENIOR DESIGNER Toni Kay
COMMISSIONING EDITOR Annabel Morgan
LOCATION RESEARCH Emily Westlake
PRODUCTION Gordana Simakovic
ART DIRECTOR Leslie Harrington
EDITORIAL DIRECTOR Julia Charles

First published in 2012
by Ryland Peters & Small
20–21 Jockey's Fields,
London WC1R 4BW
and
519 Broadway, 5th Floor
New York, NY 10012

10 9 8 7 6 5 4 3 2 1

Library of Congress Cataloging-in-Publication Data

Pentreath, Ben.
English decoration : timeless inspiration for the contemporary home / Ben Pentreath ; with a foreword by Nicky Haslam ; photography by Jan Baldwin Ryland. -- First [edition].
pages cm
Includes index.
ISBN 978-1-84975-266-4
1. Interior decoration--England--Themes, motives.
I. Title.
NK2043.P46 2012
747.0942--dc23
2012018117

A catalogue record for this book is available from the British Library.

Printed in China

CONTENTS

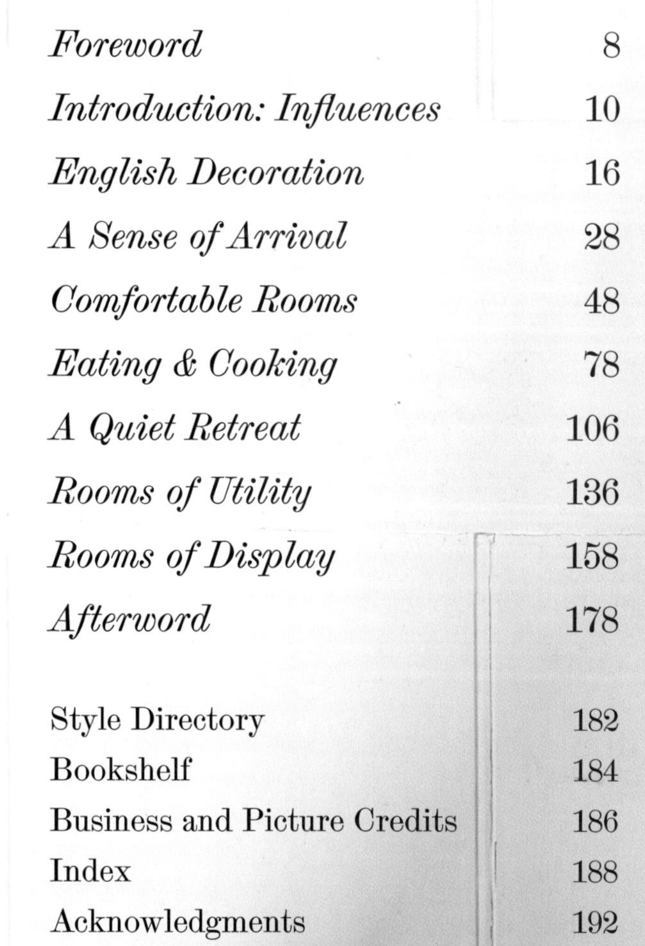

DAVID
HOCK
Fleurs fraiches

FOREWORD

IT IS ENTIRELY POSSIBLE that Ben Pentreath is the creation of P. G. Wodehouse come vividly alive and magically teleported into the here and now. As a 'Plum' character, he would be totally at home against a backdrop of aunts in draughty country houses, prickly tweed suits, groaning grog trays and spaniel-swarming gun rooms, mahogany thunderboxes, gigantic porcelain bathtubs, many-horned trophies, corridor-creeping and ear trumpets. But in fact there is nothing of the indolent toff about him. Pentreath is a human dynamo, a designer and draughtsman who runs a prolific architectural practice and a delectable boutique in Bloomsbury. He has natural ebullience and enormous charm and could only be English, though wisely he widened his visual appreciation and honed his professional ethic in *mondain* Manhattan.

Twenty-first-century comfort, clear colours and skilful restraint are paramount in the rooms Ben has chosen for this book, but he's noticed a dash of unobtrusive humour and unique style in all of them. His own work is influenced by, but never imitative of, past masters such as David Hicks, whose seminal *Living With Design* lies atop Ben's coffee table. Like Hicks, he improves everything he touches, combining the best of the old and the finest of the new, although 'the next big thing' is not his bag. Ben is, at heart, too much of a Romantic to chuck out what is old and beautiful, tried, tested and time-warmed, merely to follow a fashion. Gilt, luxe and opulence are not his thing, he prefers a misty glow to eye-watering dazzle. It's illuminating to read Ben's memories of his childhood, which, Proust-like, still inform and influence his reactions to rooms, houses and places.

Ben's preferences are refreshingly unpretentious. He likes his buildings with patina: worn flagstones or tiles, kibbled brickwork, a little bit of mess and a lot of moss. Just as every proper Englishman grows up loving Nanny and having custard with his pudding, Ben has singled out the rooms that epitomize this home-grown style; a fusion of careful planning—or indeed, happily, sometimes none—natural lighting and judicious selectiveness overlaid with the slow accretions of time and tradition.

There is also a delightful whiff of austerity about his choices; a precedent set by hazy prep-school memories of linoleum, freezing dormitories and even colder baths. Thus, we see here a paean of praise to the utility room, that ubiquitous *necessitas* of every house in town or country, the place where flower vases, tennis rackets, outdoor shoes and riding crops can be tidily tucked away or artlessly arranged. Ben has an enduring bias against the 'fitted' kitchen; his tendency is towards one like that at Garsington Manor with its many-shelved Victorian dresser painted the lemon-yellow of a finch's wing. But the grand and the modern have their moment here too, with homage paid to the Camden Town house of artist David Gentleman and his wife Sue, a temple of 1970s modernism *à la* Conran that somehow manages to be both chic and retro.

Ben's ability to put together a room manifests itself in both his homes, with just the right number of comfortable chairs, pictures in harmony and that sudden injection of vibrant colour—a turquoise table lamp, say, or firecracker dahlias in a silver mug on his rectory fireplace, in direct reference to William Nicholson. Indeed, he shares with Nicholson a confident eye for the prettiest paint colours in appropriate places, *vide* the ointment pink walls in his own Fitzrovia flat and the apple green writing room belonging to my friend A. N. Wilson, a chrome yellow entrance hall in Suffolk and the more golden version that transforms a rather dank basement corridor in north London.

These, and the many other interiors, illustrate Ben's historical appreciation, lighthearted romanticism and sense of authentic beauty, which make every room he admires, or decorates, a perfect setting for its occupants. And with this book, Ben takes us on a ravishing journey through the realms of his diverse, yet impeccable, taste.

Nicky Haslam, London 2012

HOTEL ALGONQUIN
NEW YORK

INTRODUCTION
Influences

WHEN I WAS VERY YOUNG, I used to play for hours in an old stone barn at the back of our garden, in West Dorset. It is one of the first rooms I can recall with clarity. I loved its smells and dusty shelves filled with old clay flowerpots and spiders' webs. I can remember that shed intensely, although I have not been in it for over thirty years.

What is it about our memory that it is intertwined so strongly with recollections of places, smells, rooms, I wonder—as much, or in fact more so, than people? From time to time, I must confess, I meet someone at a party who says 'How are you? I haven't seen you in thirty years!' And I have absolutely no idea if I've ever met him in my life. Yet I can still remember vividly the buildings of the old country house on the borders of Dorset and Wiltshire where we went to school when we were eight. I used to practise piano in an oak-panelled room on the first floor of the handsome Georgian stair hall. The walls were lined with mahogany cases containing thousands of butterflies, moths and insects, collected in the nineteenth century by the famous General Pitt Rivers who had once owned the house and park. Needless to say, I was much more interested in the butterflies than the piano, and I never got particularly far with learning to read music. Very recently I have bought a beautiful old nineteenth-century piano, in faded burr walnut, and I am wondering if I can do any better now?

MY GRANDPARENTS, in the 1950s, built a house overlooking the Beaulieu River in Hampshire. Having bought their plot of land, they couldn't afford much for the house; so it was a fairly simple wooden bungalow, with shingle walls and wide glass walls overlooking the woods and the river. I used to love staying there.

My grandmother had been very influenced by the Festival of Britain when decorating her house. There were many Festival fabrics, and prints by John and Paul Nash in the bedrooms. My bedroom was named 'Haystacks' after the picture of John Nash's famous painting of that name. The dining room ceiling was painted a rich purple, and my grandfather's study was lined with books and his collection of Greek antiquities, and painted a deep Pompeian red.

They had arrived in England at the end of the war, after ten years in South Australia, without furniture but with a large, cold headmaster's house in Shropshire to move into and furnish. My grandmother set about visiting country house auctions and snapping up the old brown furniture that was not at all in fashion. The combination of modern textiles and good, plain, inexpensive Georgian furniture is something that I think I might have learned from her, and I love it to this day.

When I was seventeen, at school, I made such a nuisance of myself that I was allowed to join a rather exclusive small boarding house located in an old block that had originally been built to house the estate gardeners. Now it was the home of pupils who, for one reason or another, were not particularly well suited to the rigorous life of boarding houses. For my part, I think I'd just had enough of the regime—compounded when my intelligent, civilized housemaster (I am still friends with him and his wife) retired to make way for a younger, more strident model, who also had the misfortune to teach me science.

Each room was painted white and had bare wooden floorboards and a simple Victorian sash window. It had a small, very plain fireplace and I can still remember, on the mantelshelf, having a pair of white china and brass candlesticks, and on the windowsill growing a pair of white geranium plants (something else that I love to this day). Although I didn't know it at the time, being in this room was exactly like living in a watercolour painted by Eric Ravilious.

A couple of years later I was a student at the University of Edinburgh, where I read History of Art. I gravitated inexorably towards the great grey New Town, where for my last two years I lived with four friends in a huge early nineteenth-century flat in Abercrombie Place. It had a tall, double-height stair hall with an extraordinary stone staircase—the sort of flat that you dream about, and which passes into legend. I have recently had the great pleasure of spending some time working in Edinburgh, and rediscovering that remarkable city twenty years later. I am not sure I have ever lived in such a handsome room as during those two years. The fireplace was classic Adam, made of pine with cast gesso decorations; there was a plaster cornice, and a broad sash window overlooking green and stone rear gardens with tall New Town houses opposite.

I moved into the flat with my great friend Jane, who twenty years later, with her husband Johnny Holland, is slowly restoring a farm near to me in West Dorset—and creating what will be the most idyllic paradise you have seen. Thinking back, we were really very young in those days. I remember us organizing a painting party when we first took possession. The place was very tired and a little unloved. Not a lot of painting happened, but a lot of very cheap red wine was drunk. Eventually everyone left, and over two weeks Jane and I got it sorted. A year later our friend Hugo joined the flat. The building was freezing in winter, but in the summer the three of us used to clamber out of the attic windows onto a small flat roof and eat supper looking at the sun setting across the rooftops of

PREVIOUS PAGE A corner of my sitting room in London. The framed map was drawn in 1746 by John Rocque and fills the entire wall above my sofa. The City of London appears in the upper panels, and was so small in those days that one could have walked from St Paul's to the fields at the edge of the city in about half an hour. I like the fact that Great Ormond Street, where I live, was already built and is shown on the map. A lamp by Marianna Kennedy, a woven silk cushion by Alpa Mistry and Wedgwood Sheringham candlesticks by Ronald Stennett-Willson provide bold touches in an otherwise muted palette. The turquoise of the lampshade is one of my favourite colours.

RIGHT Me, aged three. I am not entirely sure how happy I am to be photographed, at the Beaulieu River by my grandparents' house, in a sweater knitted by my mother.

Georgian Edinburgh; dreaming of what the future would bring, and watching, on rare warm evenings, the sky, sea and clouds merging into a golden Firth of Forth.

I graduated from Edinburgh and moved to Norfolk, where I worked for the architect Charles Morris. He taught me a huge amount about those magic ingredients that make a house sing and a garden flow, and about the emotive qualities of materials and architecture; and showed by brilliant example that, in order to be right, everything must be put together with consummate care.

In the local village, I rented a tiny cottage down a long lane, surrounded by fen and woodland. It was called 'The Hideaway'. Appropriately, the rooms were incredibly small and had mere six-foot high ceilings. It was here that my landlady Caro, who lived in London at the time but would come and stay at weekends, set about turning the two-acre wilderness into an extraordinary garden and taught me to re-love gardening for the first time since I had my own small vegetable patch at home when I was six. There is nothing in the world so satisfying as making a garden; my greatest pleasure is now restoring the garden around my own house in Dorset—but that is another story.

From this remote Norfolk cottage I moved, when I was 27, to New York. That enormous change was mitigated by my finding, with a lot of luck and some perserverance, a minute flat on the top floor of a beautiful, crumbling 1820s townhouse in Greenwich Village. My cousin Ben came to stay and we ripped up the grim carpet and scrubbed the floorboards. I painted the walls—first a pale grey and then a year later, in the middle of a very cold New York winter, a strong Chinese yellow. My bedroom walls I wallpapered using tea-stained photocopies from a book of botanical engravings. The Greek Revival fireplace drew perfectly, and for my first two years in New York City, this little apartment on Bank Street was my nest.

I was working around the corner, in the then unrestored Meatpacking District, for Fairfax & Sammons, one of the small but powerful and growing band of traditional architects now practising in the United States. Richard and Anne taught me an enormous amount, both about architecture and business, but probably the greatest influence of all was just living for five years in hectic, beautiful New York City.

When it was time to leave Bank Street, I moved to a narrow railroad apartment on King Street, where the Village meets Soho. It was what they call a 'six-storey walk-up', which was no joke if you forgot something on your way out of the house, but being on the top floor it had extraordinary views on three sides and I used to wake up and go to sleep every day looking across the New York skyline to the Empire State Building. It was in this little apartment that I first experimented with a few strong fabrics and some contemporary furniture alongside old brown tables and chairs, and loved the results.

When I moved back to London in the autumn of 2003, with tears in my eyes but nonetheless so happy to be coming home, I rented a small, panelled early Georgian flat in Bloomsbury. It is another tiny place, but it suits me brilliantly. Around the corner I subsequently opened my architectural office, and then more recently our shop in a little pair of Victorian shops on Rugby Street.

I have been here for nine years now, and it is a part of London that I love—not least, I have to admit, because I have been lucky enough to combine living here with taking a long lease on a plain, unrestored 1820s parsonage in West Dorset. Here I have been able to escape, and have both the time and space really to make a garden.

All of these places and experiences have, I think, gone to define my approach to decoration. They are all quite simple spaces and (with the exception of the parsonage and Edinburgh) very small indeed. But they all had character and they all have had a spirit of quiet contentment. Obviously, I've worked at putting them together in this way or that; but never too much, in a way that feels forced or, I hope, over-precious. This is really the subject of my book.

Ben Pentreath
Great Ormond Street, London, 2012

RIGHT Another corner of my sitting room in London. I stripped layers of paint from the early eighteenth-century chimneypiece, revealing cool, flat grey marble. The shelf would have been added later, but is useful—I am not a purist, so it stays. A Hans Wegner CH25 lounge chair sits comfortably next to an early Georgian chest of drawers, and a Moroccan Beni Ouarain rug provides a cosy touch.

THE HOUSES OF IRELAND
TOWN PLANNING IN LONDON
THE ENGLISH TOWN
TOWN AND COUNTRY
Early Georgian Interiors
THE SEARCH FOR A STYLE
Irish houses & castles
LATE GEORGIAN
MID GEORGIAN
EARLY GEORGIAN
THE VICTORIAN COUNTRY HOUSE

CHAPTER I

English Decoration

WHAT IS IT THAT gives English rooms such character, so that we can know them as well as people; like them and love them; belong in them; feel at ease with them?

There is a mysterious alchemy in the putting together of rooms and houses. Myriad ingredients combine to create the perfect interior: light, views, the relationship of one room to the next, and to the landscape or city beyond; furniture and rugs; books and lamps; plants and flowers; sounds—the ticking of a clock, or the deep, still silence of an old room in the country; and scents—of garden roses, or woodsmoke. Or maybe it is the personality of the owner that is strongest, woven into every fibre?

These are the ingredients of all the best English rooms. The ways in which they are best combined is the theme that we will return to time and again. And, rather like cooking, achieving some results can be as simple as following a recipe. In the process of writing this book, I have thought carefully about these recipes, and how we might plan for success. As we look at each room, I will unpick what I think makes it special. Like the best food, sometimes one must keep it simple and light; elsewhere, richness and ornament have their part to play. Often, luck has a role. But above all, the most magical—and, of course, elusive—constituent of English decoration is gentle, slow-roasted time.

A HOUSE IN THE COUNTRY. On one façade, overlooking the garden, and facing southwest towards the view, tall sash windows with slender glazing bars allow the afternoon light to stream into a faded drawing room.

Softly patterned grey wallpaper is hung with prints and old oil paintings in dark gilt frames; here and there, the memory of a picture removed leaves a shadow on the wall where the gentle floral pattern can be read more clearly.

From distant beech trees a wood pigeon calls its song of summer. A bee drowsily meanders in through the open window and finds its way out again, into a garden scented with old cream roses, delphiniums and lilies. The wool carpet, the colour of washed tobacco, moth-eaten at its perimeter, is overlaid with richly coloured Turkey and Persian rugs, collected and laid down in another era.

The sofa is covered in a simple, fresh blue and white cotton ticking. Deep cushions in scarlet and small leaf-covered prints provide comfort and a splash of colour. An ottoman is piled with interesting books, and in front of a window sits a pair of Regency cane chairs, next to their own small reading table. A dog is fast asleep on an armchair. The scent of potpourri combines with the smell of woodsmoke from centuries of fires.

What is it about this description that lets us know at once that we are in an English room; that we are not in France, say, or in Italy, Holland, Germany or America? Is it the accretion of decades, the wear and tear, the imperfection, or the calm knowledge and inevitability with which these disparate things have been put together and belong? All these things, yes, and the unstudied way in which we have in an instant achieved both comfort and cosiness, grandeur and simplicity, sense and sensibility: in short, a place the English can call home.

A hundred and twenty miles from those (let us imagine) West Wiltshire downs, in North London the sound of The Beatles' *Rubber Soul* fills the tall stairway of a late Georgian house in Camden. The walls are painted an electric, cobalt (or so-called Reckitt's) blue. The front door is bright canary gloss; the walls in the basement kitchen a dark burnt orange. Bicycles are propped in the hallway and nineteenth-century printed playbills decorate the walls.

The downstairs lavatory is wallpapered in a psychedelic re-colouring of a William Morris wallpaper. On the first floor, the drawing room is painted white. The room is sparsely furnished. A Hockney drawing—in perfect coloured pencil—shows a vase of wilting tulips on a checked tablecloth. An old grey linen chesterfield sofa, bought from Habitat in 1978, has seen all family life come and go. Toddlers turned to teenagers on this sofa; arguments and reconciliations, family gatherings and bereavements have taken place here.

Tall double doors lead to a second, light-filled room that over the years has functioned variously as a playroom, library, TV room, study and guest bedroom. Now the book-lined walls rest quietly, the coloured spines of novels and history books, philosophy and art somewhat less read, but no less loved, than they were forty years ago. Floor-to-ceiling windows overlook a bleakly beautiful urban landscape of tower blocks and Georgian chimneys, of London plane trees and parking meters, of flight trails tracing silver threads through an autumn sky.

And what fascinates me: this amalgam of a house is every bit as English as the first—perhaps more so. How may we consider both in parallel; simultaneously yet apart? That, I think, is one question posed by this book.

Unplanned, unpremeditated; rooms in which everything individually might not be quite right, but where everything together sings perfectly; a look—a state of mind, in fact—that allows at once for the old and the new, the country and the city, for simplicity and complexity, modernity and history.

PREVIOUS PAGE A first floor library designed by my friend George Saumarez Smith. The elegant, plain bookcase has a flat 'Soane' arch at its summit, offering a touch of lightness to the weighty knowledge contained in so many books. A faded green velvet armchair provides the perfect spot to curl up for the afternoon. The faded, richly coloured Persian carpet reflects the colours of the spines of the books. In the foreground, note the simple elegance of the nickel handrail to the stairs.

LEFT Horst P. Horst's achingly beautiful photograph of John Fowler's own sitting room at The Hunting Lodge (now the home of Nicky Haslam): a masterwork of English decoration. The soft Fowler colours are given just the jolt of colour needed by the primrose yellow Howard chair and the vivid scarlet dahlias. Delicate eighteenth-century furniture is strangely at home in the humble interior.

These are the homes of the curious, messy, inimitable, paradoxical English: simultaneously occupying as we do Blake's dark Satanic Mills, and yet dreaming of his green and pleasant Land.

A survey of English decoration that starts with the history of the mediaeval hall and ends with a modernist villa, this is not. Plenty exist, yet I do not believe that we decorate our rooms, or live, as historians, in museums. Neither is my concern here those great treasure houses, the castles and palaces for which the English are renowned—extraordinary and magnificent they are, of course, but they are the homes of dukes and princes and verge themselves into galleries. Those are rooms built for display, not for living, and which, were it not for a certain casualness, a taken-for-granted indifference to their splendour, have more in common with their grand, uncomfortable continental and American counterparts than their owners might care to admit.

These pages investigate more modest houses. One or two of them, it is true, are what might be described as 'grand' modest houses; but the majority are farmhouses and vicarages, townhouses and cottages. It is here that my heart belongs, and, I believe, the heart of the English when they think of home. There are houses in richly layered corners of London, and beautiful, sometimes remote, patches of England—and Wales and Scotland, too—for, as I hope to demonstrate, the English style of decoration is not quite limited by geographical boundaries, but more by a state of mind. Above all, these are the houses of friends. It has occurred to me, looking back through the photographs, seeking common threads and contrasts, that friendship is perhaps the greatest singular theme that binds them all.

"The best kind of English rooms," wrote David Hicks of his own study in 1986, "are those which contain a cosmopolitan collection of different pieces of furniture, books, drawings and objects though somehow sympathetic to each other, in a space with a decorative theme, however simple, all of which goes to make up a cosy, interesting and individual atmosphere."

This description, by my great hero (as much for his writing as for his rooms), seems to sum up in a single sentence all that is good and right about the rooms that we photographed for this book. In none of them has too much been thought about. Instead, there is an effortlessness in the way they are put together that provides the balance between just enough and too much, and between careful planning and enjoyable accidents. These are themes to which we will return time and again.

Hicks is a towering figure in my personal understanding of English decoration. Repeatedly, I turn to his books and his rooms when pondering a problem or considering new ways of doing things. He had a knack of understanding the balance between harmony and discord that feels unique among the twentieth-century decorators. Where everything is pretty, he injects a note of shock; where in danger of becoming too formal, he suggests a subtle dressing-down brought in by a modern piece of furniture, or art, or lighting.

I am not sure his look should, or can, be imitated. Some have tried, but it was his, and I doubt it can be repeated. Hicks occupied a perfect combination of time and place; he had the houses, the eye, the money and the boldness to create gloss scarlet or puce walls in grand country houses that in later, more timid (yet probably more sensitive) decades would seem anathema.

He was of the time that understood and relished the vigour of modernity; and yet simultaneously realized what the underbelly of that same modernity tended to destroy. "I am particularly interested," he wrote, "in preserving those beautiful parts of England which are threatened daily by new developments and building. Almost all are ill-considered and badly sited, but I sometimes feel it is completely wasted energy even being interested in preservation or good modern architecture. Under our eyes every village, small town and city is being villainously wrecked." Writing, as I am, at a distance of 43 years, it is depressing how similar our concerns are today. *Plus ça change, plus c'est la même chose.*

RIGHT Here is my hero, David Hicks, at home in Oxfordshire. Pumpkin soup walls have a thick brown border; a bold portrait watches over one of Hicks's famous tablescapes, carefully arranged on a Chippendale Gothick table that is at once brittle yet robust. Glimpsed through the open doorway, David Hicks's fantastic chocolate brown study, warmed with richly toned leather book spines arranged (classic Hicks) neither by author or subject, but by colour.

Lodge Simla

POOR COOK

Perhaps for this reason we should not be surprised how deeply runs the theme of preservation in the history of English taste. Maybe this is why I never feel my architectural work belongs on a shelf of its own, but that it forms part of and belongs to a continuous whole. The desire to repair, to recreate, is a deep, great, repetitive drumbeat of our national architectural history, which found its expression in the eighteenth-century Jacobean revivals, in the nineteenth-century battle of styles and, differently, in the Arts and Crafts of William Morris, Lutyens, Barnsley and Gimson. Even in English Modernism, that curious affair, I find in the work of all the best of our architects the same deep-tolling relationship to land and to place, to material and materiality, that conditions all our earlier great artistic and architectural endeavours.

The havoc of post-war upheaval, of the huge, shuddering earthquake of social change that brought about the destruction of the country house, the violation of our great cities and the unprecedented crisis of confidence (that seems, to me, to have peaked roughly when I was two years old, in 1973)—this havoc has, over the past forty years or so, received a balm; a better understanding of the past, and our land, and our history, and a respect for it. But is the danger today that we treat history too carefully; that in attempting to preserve what we value, we destroy it, via a process of framing, conserving, placing under glass and of cloying over-explanation?

Into this world steps David Mlinaric, another hero, who poises with perfect balance—avoiding the kiss of death of too much visible knowledge, while simultaneously having all of the knowledge required to create his precise, measured, quietly perfect version of English historical decoration: rooms that we know must never quite have existed, yet distil in their entirety a complete and heady essence of the past. Together with his fellow 'History Boys'—the antiques dealers and makers of taste Piers von Westenholz, Robert Kime and Christopher Gibbs—Mlinaric sought to reintegrate the pretty, delicate language of John Fowler with a more robust nineteenth-century aesthetic. No survey of English decoration is complete without an understanding of Fowler, and his extraordinary achievements, yet I confess to preferring the richer additions of William IV and Victoria to Fowler's fine Regency consommé.

The result is a stronger and more heady soup, one that I find intoxicating, which rediscovered pleasure in nineteenth-century oak and plain eighteenth-century brown furniture, in Turkey carpets and bare scrubbed floorboards, in old cupboards and tapestries, and large-scale Victorian landscapes in heavy gilt frames; black gothic lamps and bold glazed chintzes, in Ravilious and Paul Nash. This is the world of Parson Kilvert, of strong Irish colours, of longevity and tradition in the face of so much destruction encountered, first hand, in the Britain of the late 1960s and early 1970s. It is a world that encounters and brings to vivid life a precious past, elegiac yet never mournful. In a new generation, it is a world brought to vivid life by my friends Edward Hurst, Max Rollitt and Will Fisher—those three oustanding antiques dealers who we might like to think of as the History Boys of today. And this is the world where I feel I begin, and will probably end.

And yet—other strands persist. At just the same time as Mlinaric is triumphantly redecorating Beningbrough Hall—with its muted palette of achingly beautiful greys—Terence Conran and Stafford Cliff are promoting their own version of what constitutes English decoration, in the magnificent, timeless series of Habitat catalogues that the pair produced between 1971 and 1981. Habitat, which Conran had founded a decade earlier, was quietly and brilliantly revolutionizing the English high street. Are there any more English rooms than those that Conran has created and moulded over the years at his house, Barton Court? He published his houses widely, and it was in these rooms that his revolution in our taste for good, modern, well-designed things (resting comfortably alongside antiques, old toy cars and vintage advertising material) was forged. Infinitely more democratic, more

LEFT Another hero, David Mlinaric, like Fowler and Hicks produced some of his most serene work for himself: this is a corner of Thorpe Hall, the tall Tudor house in Norfolk that David and Martha Mlinaric made their home in the 1970s. This is in the kitchen wing, and has all the ingredients I love most: limewashed timber-boarded walls, painted nineteenth-century furniture and a stack of trugs all ready for the garden. Many others would have corrected the sloping floor; David Mlinaric knows exactly what to leave alone.

concerned with contemporary life than the elegant flat paint of Mlinaric's Georgian panelling, there is nonetheless equivalence. It is a connection made by Michael Pick, writing in *The English Room*, in 1985:

"Muted backgrounds, patches of colouring in textiles, a few pieces of carefully chosen furniture, all these framed by stripped floorboards. Parallel to this approach was the look inspired by the 'Habitat' shops, with simple modern furniture and one carefully positioned 'antique'."

But, Pick warns with prescience, "both forms of decoration suffer the disadvantage of being in such good taste that they become bland." Blandness: which the English have always considered with horror, be it in their decoration, education, sporting achievement or political life. It is better to fail with distinction than be averagely invisible; something else, perhaps, that distinguishes us from our continental or American cousins, and yet which contributes so greatly to the innate make-up of so many rooms in this book.

If we are looking for a unifying strand in the work of all these richly varied exponents of the English 'Look'—Conran and Mlinaric, Kime, Hicks or Fowler—one might be that their best achievements are always their own rooms and houses. Did Hicks ever decorate as richly as at Britwell Salome or The Grange? Did Fowler ever design as beautifully as his own Hunting Lodge? (now lived in by that great, bold and happy mind of English decoration today, Nicky Haslam, who has written the foreword to this book). I still remember, when I was seventeen years old, encountering Horst P. Horst's extraordinary photographs of these rooms for the first time; they are still able to send a shiver down my spine.

Occasionally, just for a moment in our lives, there is a perfect balance between decorator and client—at which point we can create great things. But the English, while they may be happy for a bit of help picking the curtains or wallpaper, are innately suspicious of 'Interior Decoration'. Another unifying theme of these pages, then, is that none of the rooms photographed has seen the hand of a professional interior designer. Of all facets of the English style, I think this is the one that Americans find hardest to understand, although it was an American, Nancy Lancaster, who remarked, with great understatement, "I'm agin decoration: I'm just a percolator of ideas". English decoration is about finding your own voice, discovering your own confidence, and not merely about meekly receiving the taste of others.

Above all, English decoration relates to her light and her landscape. The gloom of London is banished by the apple green joinery of Andrew Wilson's study, or in my own case, by the warm pink walls of my panelled sitting room. The extraordinary, brilliant yellow walls that announce the hall at the opening of Chapter II (see pages 30–31) expel the flat white light of the Suffolk countryside. And the walls of Garsington envelop us in a comfortable, ageless, soft oak-smoked embrace.

A friend, documenting recently the manufacture of Harris Tweed, noted how the colours and texture of the northern landscape find themselves woven into the warp and weft of every piece of that cloth. Exactly the same might be said of these English rooms. At once of all time, and of now, of all places, and of their own, they present a fleeting example of that most universal—and paradoxically disparate—of styles: the many worlds of English decoration.

RIGHT Four aspects of English decoration. Clockwise from above left: A delicate, timeworn painted cane sofa (in the manner of William Morris) at Garsington Manor in Oxfordshire—creamy and dreamy against dark oak panelling. The soft cushions and kelims provide a comfortable touch. Above right: Peter Hone's splendid Notting Hill bathroom—a paradigm of the English gentleman's room, with its old Gothick pine cupboard and rich red walls, and plaster casts crammed into corners and filling every last surface. Below right: A spare, stripped-back landing at Chris and Caddy Wilmot-Sitwell's Dorset home; the oculus window that we see on page 33 set into a simple timber-lined opening. The Georgian tripod table has stubby legs; the red geranium extends toward the sunlight; plain scrubbed boards reflect the light. Below left: I have hung a bold Josef Frank textile from Svenskt Tenn across the back of my bed at my own flat in London. Combined with a vivid Marianna Kennedy lamp and bright linen from Olatz in New York, it provides a colourful foil to the sombre oak frame of the four-poster bed that I inherited from my grandparents.

OVERLEAF Rusting nineteenth-century railings and an elegant metal gate overlook a corner of untouched parkland in Suffolk. Sheep safely graze under ancient oaks. The midsummer air is heavy with the threat of later rain. The sound of crickets and bees fills the air. This scene, too, might be a fragment from a dream.

The right sort.
TO THE CRACK RIDERS OF ENGLAND.

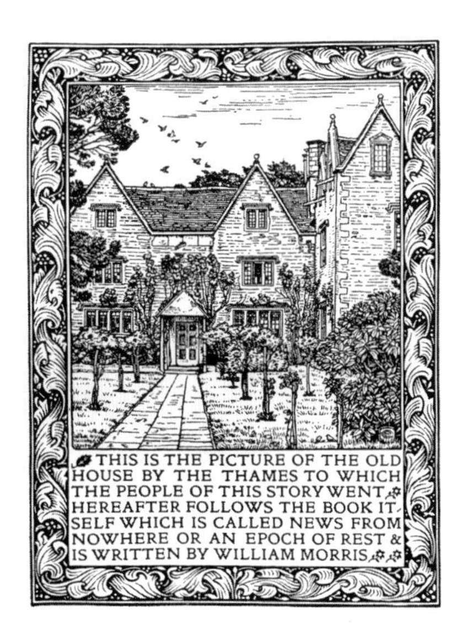

CHAPTER II
A Sense of Arrival

THE WOODCUT ABOVE illustrates the opening page of William Morris's *News from Nowhere*. 'This is the Picture,' he writes, 'of the old house by the Thames to which the people of this story went. Hereafter follows the book itself, which is called News from Nowhere or An Epoch of Rest'. A plain stone path is bounded on both sides by mossy lawn with standard roses growing from neatly cut discs of earth.

The path leads directly to the door of a handsome, gabled, grey-golden stone house—Kelmscott Manor, in Oxfordshire, which Morris used as a summer retreat. I wonder if a greater portrayal of English domesticity has ever been produced? Nothing suggests a sense of generous welcome as much as this garden path. A modest approach heightens my anticipation more than the gate lodge and drive of a great country house. While I love the drama of the latter, I confess to preferring a brick path, lined with spring bulbs and box trees, leading to the boarded door of a cottage or the panelled porch of a rectory.

A glazed fanlight is above the door, each facet of glass catching the light so as to give sparkle and life to the whole; pale polished brassware, rubbed to a gleaming whiteness for generations, with a small smudge of grey-green polish on the adjacent brickwork; the door painted a soft colour, and left ajar, allowing us a glimpse to the hall beyond as we pull the bell-cord and announce our arrival to distant corridors.

IN MY MIND we should seek in our houses a spirit of kind welcome. Buildings become home when filled with friends and family. The front door and hall is where we invite them in.

Walls might be panelled, in oak or painted wood, or in simple cottages with beaded boards; or painted plaster in strong colours, or papered with bold patterns. I like halls to be hung with prints and maps, and over-scaled dark oil paintings. This is our palette.

Keep furniture sparse: pairs of hall chairs in dark mahogany or pale pickled oak, perhaps; a useful, deep, stone-topped table with a china bowl that becomes home to dog leads, car keys and letters—transitory objects on their way to rooms and places more permanent. There are handy baskets in one corner, pink geraniums overwintering, a scattering of coats and boots that have not yet made their way to back offices. This is the English hall.

Floors should always be practical and hardwearing: stone flags, polished by centuries of comings and goings. Only grander houses should have patterned stonework; with diamond corners picked out in a contrasting slate, or using soft grey and white marble squares. For simpler houses, stone slabs laid with tight butt joints (never with visible mortar) in a broad, coursed pattern are best. The stone should be local. My own house, The Old Parsonage, has a beautiful hall floor of Blue Lias limestone laid straight onto the earth. Cottages would have floors of humbler materials still; brick or terracotta—similarly, never laid with fat cement mortar joints, which always betray a modern touch, and always look wrong.

In London townhouses, an austere exterior of soot-black brick gives way to rich plasterwork or panelling, the door and fanlight providing the tiniest hint of the richness to come. Early Georgian fanlights have sturdy patterns in thick timber glazing bars; a hundred years later, refined leaded light patterns reflect the delicacy of the Regency, mass produced in their day. Furniture, by necessity, is neater and tighter in the confines of the city; perhaps just a narrow hall table with a stone top and tall mercury glass mirror above, to reflect light about the interior. In the country, we can be more generous. A round hall table is filled with a bunch of June roses, fresh from the garden, diffusing the boundaries between inside and out.

Beyond the hall is the staircase, and here, perhaps, the mood may soften further still; stone floors give way to oak, or plaster walls to panelling. The staircase encapsulates the story of architectural history more beautifully, perhaps, than any other room in the house; from the elaborate oak creations of the Jacobean house, with fantastical carvings and heraldic ornament, myth and legend encapsulated in stone and timber, via the generation of Wren, with richly turned balusters, fat handrails and timeworn oak treads, to the light delicacy of the eighteenth century, whose mission, it seems, was to make the staircase to appear as if it hardly touched the ground. Then there is the staircase in the Arts and Crafts house, whose architects take us on planned routes through the building, with small windows at special corners opening up vistas across distant valleys.

Halls and staircases give us opportunity to decorate in ways that may not work in other, less transitory spaces. We can be bold. Because we pass in and out but never linger, strong patterns and colours are at home in hallways and stairs, putting a smile on our faces as we go. One of my favourite rooms is the bright yellow hall in the house in Suffolk shown on the previous pages. I cherish that extraordinary colour, banishing as it does any sense of disquiet from this happiest and most relaxed of homes.

PAGE 28 AND PREVIOUS PAGES Light floods into this extraordinary hall in a Neoclassical country house in Suffolk and is reflected from every surface—the glazed prints and pictures, the glass-fronted bookcases and the ancient stone-flagged floor. A rocking horse sits waiting quietly for young riders; antlers prove testament to previous generations' travels to Scotland. But the masterstroke is the saturated yellow walls, painted in the early 1960s. Today's more timid generation might choose a subtle grey from Farrow & Ball. How dull this vibrant room would be in comparison!

RIGHT In west Dorset, a simple stone path leads to the humble panelled door of an elegant stone farmhouse. '1706' reads the date stone above the door; the broad sash windows would have been fitted much later, but the *oeil-de-boeuf* window above reveals this earlier origin. The white painted gate, with its delicate handle and curved top, is pleasing in its neat simplicity. But most powerful of all is the direct connection through the front door and hallway to the brilliant green of the walled orchard beyond. What greater sense of inviting welcome could we imagine?

1706

ABOVE Most beautiful of all, perhaps, is this wonderful painted surface. When Chris and Caddy Wilmot-Sitwell stripped back the old walls, they found this splendid decoration beneath; warm earth colours that one suspects will have been mixed straight from the local clays and pigments. A piquant note is provided by the horizontal band of cloudy ultramarine blue. When the house needed restoring, rising damp was found all around. The existing walls had to be chopped back to a height of three feet, and replastered with a soft, breathable traditional lime plaster. There is an archaeology to this room, therefore, that would be impossible to invent, but which is irresistible to keep.

LEFT We have entered the hall of the Wilmot-Sitwell's Dorset farmhouse shown on the previous page. The interior is revealed to be a cool space—elegant yet with virtually no architecture: just lime-plastered walls, a simple staircase, a plain enamel pendant light and a stone-topped hall table. Light falls softly on the coursed stone-flagged floor. Note how the stones are tightly butt-jointed; a traditionally laid floor should never have visible mortar joints. It is polished and rubbed by the footfall of ages. This room would still be recognized by the farmers who lived here two hundred years ago. It has a timelessness that is as English as any grander example.

ABOVE LEFT In the same hall, a plain Georgian door has endured the knocks and bangs of centuries. Wisely the owners decided not to repaint it, but to leave the chips and dings in the old white gloss paintwork. You can see where the architrave has been patched at the lower right-hand corner; the old mouldings have been matched perfectly by a carpenter. Beyond the sitting room is the kitchen. A map of Dorset hangs on the wall, below the old kitchen clock; a brilliant flash of primrose yellow on the gloss-painted chair is a happy, fresh touch in a scene that in every other respect could be straight out of a painting by Vermeer.

ABOVE The entrance court of Iain and Zara Milligan's stone and limewashed house in Scotland is filled with exuberant, lush planting—testament to Zara's brilliance as a plantswoman and gardener. One stone-flagged path leads to the front door, hidden entirely under boughs of climbing roses in the far corner; the other to the wide, stone-arched back door in the foreground.

LEFT A wider view of the same stone-arched entrance. Designed in 1995 by the architect Charles Morris, this house is, I believe, one of his finest works. Everything about it resolves to perfection. Here is a perfect transition space between house and garden of which Charles is the master. A wide, generous arch welcomes us in, and provides shelter. Local red sandstone has been worked and tooled to create texture. An ancient green painted garden bench provides a perfect resting post for putting on wellington boots or piling up garden tools. Hats and shoes hang off antlers. The softly pink-stuccoed walls and 'della Robbia' plaque provide a little hint of Italy, a breath of warm southern air in the damp greenness of Dumfriesshire.

ABOVE We are looking up into the vaulted and domed stair hall of the house in Suffolk that opens this chapter. What an extraordinary scene is this—almost as if we are looking up into heaven itself. Finely detailed Greek revival plasterwork sings in different tones of white and grey to create a marvellous, balanced, symmetrical composition that is almost abstract in its qualities.

LEFT The old brass door handle in the entrance hall of the same house. The mahogany is scratched and timeworn, the chased and moulded brasswork polished by the use of ages. This door handle encapsulates that quality of 'slow-roasted time' that I love most of all about the English house. You cannot make it up; but you can set things up to be ready. Never finish wood with a shiny modern varnish; never used lacquered brass, which cannot grow old gracefully, but merely chip and tarnish badly with age. The right ingredients left to cook will create that perfect patina sooner than you can imagine.

RIGHT The same stair hall; an aristocratic assemblage of ancient family portraits, old landscapes in gilt frames, the collections of decades (old botanical drawings hung in rows, a beautiful marble 'Dying Gaul' irreverently tucked into the shadows under the stair, a giant clam shell, the figurehead from a nineteenth-century ship), tables laden with magazines and scientific journals, revealing the interests of the owner. A grand piano provides music on high days and holidays. But my favourite touch of all? The small blue tricycle, which brings a sense of vivid, happy life to the grandeur of the scene.

LEFT Layers of polished wood upon wood in the hall at Garsington Manor, the home of Mrs Rosalind Ingrams and her family. The light plays across each surface with a chiaroscuro gleam. We are enveloped by these smoky tones; by the colour of the early burr walnut chest-on-legs against the darker oak walls, and the richer brown still of the mahogany long-case clock. The gilt-metal clock face, ancient mirror and crystal chandelier provide sparkling moments that lift the scene. The liveliest touch comes from the blue and white Delft tiles of the candle sconce. I have a fascination with blue and white china—a vital ingredient of most English rooms.

ABOVE A wider view of the same hall, revealing the handsome leaded light windows and friendly oculus above the garden door. A primrose yellow sofa invites us to sit by the fire; richly coloured rugs form a patchwork on the floor. This room responds to an earlier, historic role, when the hall was the centre of the house; a place for staying, not just for coming and going. I love the rich embroidered tablecloth, which links us to other worlds, of Jacobean houses, and the tapestries of William and May Morris. Garsington has that transportative quality, a house so rich in history that as soon as we step beyond its threshold we are taken to other times and places.

ABOVE In David and Sue Gentleman's London house just off Regent's Park, the narrow early nineteenth-century staircase runs the full height of the tall four-storey townhouse. The slender handrail and delicate balusters have a Regency lightness; light streams in through tall windows. The Gentlemen have carpeted the house in a soft grey wool that is plain and practical; David's beautiful and brilliant prints line the walls.

ABOVE LEFT George Saumarez Smith's Bakelite telephone sings with the red candles in his Winchester hallway, a bright moment against the subdued blue-grey walls. A bold linocut by the architect Quinlan Terry hangs above the stair and the small, plain Georgian hall table—my favourite sort of furniture (and, in this instance, bought from my shop!).

LEFT At 3 Fournier Street, an early Georgian house in Spitalfields, a staircase of a hundred years earlier. The handrail has a satisfyingly tactile quality; turned balusters and carved newel posts reveal a richer architectural history; light falls softly on worn oak treads and against panelling painted a drab grey. A dazzling modern touch—Marianna Kennedy at her finest—comes from the cast resin plaques made in rainbow colours by Peter Hone.

RIGHT The entrance hall of this Suffolk manor house, owned by an architect with a finely balanced eye, provides a placid scene of English domesticity. A nineteenth-century hall chair and long-case clock rest against faux stone-painted walls; coats and hats line the hallway to the kitchen. Rugs cover old pine boards; a brass hall light, of the type made by Robert Kime, has a warm tone. We are in the world of the English rectory or country house: a scene in which nothing disturbs the quiet, harmonious contentment.

ABOVE An early work of a distinguished classical architect, this architectural hallway makes nods to both a classical past and to the pared-down, early modern aesthetic of the period. The scheme—otherwise muted, with pale apricot walls, ticking curtains and a traditional mahogany hall chair—is emboldened by the classical bust of a matron on a monumental marble plinth, itself relating to the two dramatic Roman busts shown on the facing page. A Biedermeier mirror reflects the doors to the garden; note the finesse of the glazing bars and the slender bolt fastening them closed. The grey Yorkstone paving is laid perfectly. If only the simple yet elegant oval brass light switches were still available today.

ABOVE Just glimpsed through the doorway in the photograph above left, the stone stairs curve elegantly on plan—a geometry displayed by the curved painted timber panelling below, and reflected by the second curve of the polished mahogany handrail as it wreaths down to a scroll. Note the way in which the stone treads meet the windowsill—everything in this house has been thought about by the young architect, and resolved. The simple door with its brass knob leads to a cloakroom beyond. The marbled wallpaper completes a period picture: a house lovingly cherished by the current owners, whose restoration of its simple, beautifully designed spaces has fully brought the house to life, both in detail and, more importantly, in character.

RIGHT A vaulted, architectural space creates presence and dramatic effect from the simplest of ingredients. What a difference the barrel-vaulted ceiling makes, with its cross vault opposite the door to the drawing room. But the real drama comes from the extraordinary Roman busts, sitting on porphyry red plinths. The nearest is cast with bright light from the fanlight over the door. The far bust is in the shadows, its dark profile magisterial against the brightly lit garden hall beyond. The William IV hall table is a strong piece, the colour of its veneer reflecting the ruddy tones of the porphyry, its paw feet tense and poised on the Yorkstone flag floor. A steel torch is practical, immediately to hand by the door, but has a plain 1930s aesthetic that does not break the studied, period quality of the space. The light-filled garden hall leads to a brick terrace outside, a perfect place to sit and have dinner on a warm summer's evening.

RIGHT The front entrance hall of Iain and Zara Milligan's house in the Scottish borders, which we saw on page 36–37. This part of the building was designed by Charles Morris as an extension to a nineteenth-century farmhouse, and in character takes on the feeling of an earlier hall house. The thick arched wall forms the link between the two. The walls are lined with timber panelling, painted a soft grey-blue; the plate rack displays Zara Milligan's collection of blue and white plates, bought over the decades at Portobello. A drama occurred one year when an owl flew down the chimney; several plates were broken before the bird was captured and released. This composed scene betrays no such chaos; rather, it has the quality of a Dutch still life painting, where light and dark, form and mass are perfectly balanced. Small posies in blue and white vases offer a rich note of colour.

BELOW The same arch, viewed from the old house. Through it, we can see Charles Morris's solid, stubby yet still elegant stone columns that form a screen between the entrance hall opposite and the dining hall that is shown on page 87. In the foreground, the nineteenth-century staircase is given a strong, warm presence with the claret red stair carpet. Rugs, lamps, blue china bowls and ornate gilt frames complete the scene.

CHAPTER III
Comfortable Rooms

COMFORT IS DISTINCT from luxury and, paradoxically, I think it is found more often in simplicity than excess. Let us think of the most comfortable rooms we know, and consider what unites them.

Lack of show; the avoidance of that lurking feeling we get so often in houses in Italy, or France, that you should be wearing your most formal suit to live up to the surroundings; enclosed by stiff, gilded furniture and elaborately woven silks. No, we English like an absence of fuss, and in its place a light, harmonious language in which everything relates to each other just enough, but not too much.

The English are masters of comfortable decoration. Partly, it must be admitted, we had to learn some of the finer arts of comfort from our American cousins. Thank goodness we no longer have to shiver in icy drawing rooms or try to read by the gloom of too few light bulbs. But never is our quiet sense of satisfaction greater than when we are sprawled in a deep sofa in an English sitting room surrounded by books, magazines, flowers in vases, a generously stocked drinks tray, friends and conversation; and enveloped in that warm, benevolent embrace of continuity that lets us know that, however much strife we see in the world, the best things in life will not change.

BEETHOVEN
STRING TRIOS
VIOLA

CONSIDER FIRST the character of the room. Is it sunny and best in the mornings, or for evening use? How does it relate to the rest of the house, or the garden? Is it cosy and snug, or airy and spacious? Rooms for the daytime are best, I think, decorated in light colours and with a gentle touch. Evening rooms invite stronger earth tones, jewel-like carpets and rugs.

When thinking about sitting rooms, I begin with the sofa. It might be an ancient, squashy affair, covered in corduroy or a linen union William Morris print; or an elegant Georgian box, with blue ticking upholstery and spare, white painted legs. Other rooms require a deep, elegant Howard frame, redolent of Edwardian afternoons, while elsewhere a comforting chesterfield strikes the perfect note. It's a question of setting a mood.

I have found over the years that you cannot fight the wrong sofa. Rooms ask for furniture of a certain character. When I moved to my parsonage, the light, plain early nineteenth-century space did not seem to work with my low Howard sofa in a green tweed check—that belonged to a different language, of Victorian and Edwardian drawing rooms. So I found the yellow sofa that is on the cover of this book from my friend Max Rollitt: a handsome, plain thing, its architectural lines softened by piles of cushions. As I always say—it is more comfortable than it looks.

I like my sofas to be generous, long enough to lie on for a late afternoon snooze. I have a phobia of little bits of furniture that are too twiddly, or look as if they might collapse if you sneeze. Even in a small room, large bits of furniture ground a scheme; in my tiny flat in London, the sofa fills one entire wall and yet is never overwhelming. In Dorset, of course, there is a much greater luxury of space, and so the sofa is backed with shelves and reading lamps, and fronted by an ottoman that becomes a place for piles of books and magazines and tea trays.

Armchairs equally need to envelop and welcome. I have always loved tall-backed wing chairs. They are happiest in old manors or early Georgian panelled rooms, where we must exclude draughts and provide enclosure next to a broad bolection moulded chimneypiece. In later rooms, Howard chairs and or cane bergères sit more comfortably, allowing us to recline with a book, or lie back with cocktails for animated conversations with friends.

Rugs, cushions and textiles provide the next ingredients. Rich colours and textures soften a room and make it our home. We may prefer our floors oak boarded, a deep, dark, rich hue, or bleached pale by sunshine; I find that I am inexorably drawn to rush matting and seagrass, coir and jute: the finer the room, the plainer the surface. And onto this I layer rugs and kelims that, in the most comfortable rooms, form their own jigsaw puzzle, each one fitting perfectly to the next.

Lamps should be placed where they are needed, offering soft pools of light around a room that leaves no part too dark or—to my mind much more horrific—too brightly lit. All of us, like old furniture, look most beautiful by candelight and this is my golden rule when lighting a room. David Hicks used to line all his lampshades with pink paper to cast an even warmer glow—something I dream of copying but haven't quite found the time to do yet!

The final touches of comfort are to please our senses: musical instruments, flowers and bowls of potpourri; or to place things exactly where they are needed—a box of pencils, or of letter paper, piles of newspapers and *Private Eye* or *Country Life*, and a table carrying a drinks tray, glasses, some tonic waters and slices of lemon. It is all these things that suffuse us with such a spirit of contentment and generous goodwill that is at the heart of the best and most comfortable of English rooms.

PAGE 48 AND PREVIOUS PAGES A detail, and broad view, of the Oak Room at Garsington—one of the most beautiful rooms I know. This is a magical space. We enter it and fly lightly across the centuries, back to the Jacobean period when the stone was sawn, the oak timbers felled and this magnificent house was constructed, riding like a ship above the Thames Valley, over which the leaded light windows of this room look. Layer upon layer of family life rests here—carpets and textiles, brilliantly coloured wing chairs, bold yellow curtains and canary china coffee cups, all set against the slow, warm drumbeat of dark oak panelling and the smell of woodsmoke.

RIGHT Writer and art historian Ruth Guilding at home in London, on the first floor of a handsome Regency terraced house near Regent's Park. Guilding has an eye for combining the serious and playful as much in her homes as in her life. A silver mirrored disco ball hangs above a 'Stop the War' poster by David Gentleman; invitations and obelisks jostle for space above the restrained marble chimneypiece.

Georgie
Kitty
Meg
6
1998
NO
war on Iraq
axis of oil
brute force
friendly fire
body bags
blood price
collateral
smart bombs
orphans
imperialism
hypocrisy
heroics
quick fix
PIRANESI
VICTORIAN SCULPTURE
THE VILLA
THE ENGLISH
FOLK DANCE & SONG SOCIETY

JASPER CONRAN COUNTRY
PRIVATE EYE
Christopher Lloyd MEADOWS
TUSCAN VILLAS

habitat
REYNOLDS STONE
ENGRAVINGS

PREVIOUS PAGES This sitting room is in my own house, an early nineteenth-century parsonage in Dorset. The room has a restful feel, and, in putting it together, I wanted to keep the mood similarly quiet and light. A William IV mahogany chair responds to the box sofa opposite, with its plain painted legs, from Max Rollitt. His primrose yellow antique linen could have been made for the house, and I was happy to find an antique kelim with a similar pale yellow amongst its stripes. The ottoman is covered in a grey and white needlepoint fabric (now sadly discontinued) by Colony, and I had it made up to the right size using legs from an old wobbly footstool bought at a junk auction. Even during the English summer, damp afternoons can mean a log fire is necessary, and there is always a basket of logs and kindling ready to light a fire. I love the smell of woodsmoke lingering in this room.

ABOVE Another corner of my sitting room: a simple Regency side table has a pair of silver candlesticks and a blue china bowl filled with potpourri. Sadly the white china Wedgwood candlestick lamp, from Hector Finch, is no longer made. A Ravilious print is glimpsed above; piles of *Country Life* and *House & Garden* magazines make for perfect Sunday afternoon reading.

RIGHT Through a glass darkly: a Regency mercury glass mirror above my fireplace is dimmed with age. I love the tones of mercury glass and silver, and white china candlesticks from Wedgwood, dusty gilt frames and the eternally surprised expression of a pair of Staffordshire china dogs. Against this palette, the dark mahogany candles and richly toned dahlias and calendula make a startling bolt of colour.

KING GEORGE
HARROW SCHOOL
Henry James
Henry James
Oxford English
Oxford English
QUALITY OF MERCY
BARRY UNSWORTH
LAST MAN IN TOWER
ARAVIND ADIGA
CHINA MIÉVILLE
EMBASSYTOWN
ROY STRONG

THE POLITICS OF GOOD INTENTIONS
Winifred Wagner
FRIEDRICH NIETZSCHE
Nietzsche

LONDON
ROMANTIC POETS
T.D. TOSSWILL
Hilaire Belloc

PREVIOUS PAGES, ABOVE AND LEFT A. N. Wilson's London study. Could we conceive a more perfect English room than this, the home of the distinguished writer, broadcaster and man of letters? The apple green joinery brightens grey London days. Black and white engravings close-framed in the traditional manner tell scenes from Shakespeare by Boydell. The grey veined marble fireplace has delicate Greek revival mouldings. In the foreground, a handsome mahogany dining table carries newspapers, books, diary, clutter; yet we know that there is a controlling order underlying everything we see.

ABOVE RIGHT The tall windows of Ruth Guilding and A. N. Wilson's drawing room overlook a leafy street. A glamorous space, it is painted the softest taupe colour, which in certain lights takes on a dusky lilac hue. Framed paintings and drawings are clustered either side of the fireplace.

RIGHT Powdery green and cardinal red cushions and a leopard skin draped across the ottoman add a touch of sharp brilliance to this room; they speak of cocktails, and 1930s cigarette holders, and of fascinating conversations after lazy Sunday lunches. Beyond, a low bookcase carries a cool, elegant Arnold Machin bust of the Queen, cast in plaster, that is the familiar feature of every postage stamp used in the United Kingdom since 1966. This extraordinarily ubiquitous image of everyday life in England, with its multitude of coloured backgrounds for different denominations, is reminiscent of a tiny fragment of Wedgwood jasperware in the corner of every envelope or postcard we send.

ABOVE AND RIGHT This is a room that belongs to the long Edwardian Summer; that extraordinary first decade of the last century, created as the clouds of the Great War were darkening the horizon and the heyday of the country house was drawing to an inexorable close. Two rooms at this Neoclassical house in Suffolk were knocked together in 1915 to form this grand drawing room; a room for parties, and teas, and slumbering in wide sofas by the fire. Taking inspiration from an early eighteenth-century room at Kelburn Castle, the white painted joinery, glass-fronted china cabinet and coved ceiling were given a fresh appearance with the frames picked out in bright apple green paint. Layer upon layer of William Morris printed linen unions form a beautiful palette of colour and pattern; many of the prints are still available today from Morris & Co. Deep armchairs and slipper chairs waltz across a massive Turkey carpet as if in conversation. The brilliant touch: the apple-blossom pink geranium that catches the soft, bright Suffolk light streaming in through tall windows that look across the park.

LEFT A detail of the vibrant turquoise and lime green curtains that the owners installed in the drawing room when they inherited the house in the 1960s. They had been living in Malaysia, where they bought yards of this extraordinary fabric. The room sings with colour, as if envisioned by a modern-day William Morris on psychedelic drugs. Similar effects can be obtained today by buying cheap bolts of African wax-resist fabrics, with their intense colours and powerful visual effects.

ABOVE The owner's library in the house shown on the preceding pages. A distinguished botanist and natural historian, his room is a veritable cabinet of curiosities, knowledge bursting from every shelf. Books have taken on a geological formation, layered in strata on every surface, into which one must mine deeply to find the required text. In the foreground, two Victorian easy chairs are the sort of things that one can still pick up for a song in local auction houses. I love this period of furniture—strong, robust and unmistakably English. For a more contemporary appearance, consider upholstering such architectural pieces with bold and vibrant textiles.

RIGHT Glimpsing into the library, light streams across the bookcases seen in the photograph above. Library steps have become a repository for more books; the shelves are crammed with papers and mementos of foreign travel. This is the world of the great explorer–collectors; the lair of a latter-day Darwin. Maps, engravings and other curios are in the foreground. Do not be afraid of filling cardboard boxes with surplus papers; here, anything will do so long as it serves a purpose. But know, too, that everything also fulfils an aesthetic function. This is a look that (despite the chaos) has been considered, and where everything contributes to a magnificent whole.

ROTARY CLUB OF KUCHING
DULME
DULME
BRITISH TOMATOES
Indonesia

ABOVE Restrained simplicity in the drawing room at 3 Fournier Street. Light shines in through south-facing windows, overlooking the magnificent Hawksmoor spire of Christ Church Spitalfields, filtered by the soft pink bookcloth blinds that Marianna Kennedy sells from her wonderful studio downstairs. A lemon yellow resin lamp glows clearly on the polished Georgian table; light reflects across ancient oak floors. There is restraint yet grandeur to this room; as I wrote in the introduction, comfort is found more in simplicity than excess. Can we imagine anything happier than being crowded here, around the burning fire at one of Marianna Kennedy and Charles Gledhill's famous parties, when the whole wonderful world of East London stirs and approaches like moths to a bright light? We cannot.

LEFT To the rear of the house, this plain panelled book room is painted in a period drab colour that is relieved by the flash of bright yellow from the bookcase, and the vivid resin of the ultramarine candlesticks—both, again, from Marianna's studio. A generous, plain, square table fills the room. I love its knocks and bangs, the marks from centuries of use, wine spills and supper parties. This is furniture that has lived and is loved. I loathe over-restored, over-polished, haughtier pieces, which have dwelt too long in the showrooms of Bond Street or in Park Lane drawing rooms. How much more sympathetic and characterful is a table like this. I suppose my whole book is a plea for such things. I have long coveted this beautiful set of bobbin-backed chairs.

ABOVE My own sitting room, in London, that we saw on pages 10 and 15 in the introduction to this book. The photograph above shows a wider view of the John Rocque 'Plan of London' that covers the wall above my sofa. It was engraved on copper plates and issued in sixteen sheets, which I close-framed and hung tightly on the wall. The framing project is complicated, but it is worth the effort; the map provides absorbing visual interest without ever dominating the small room.

RIGHT I have crammed rather a lot into a tiny space. The pale pink walls were a bit of a gamble; when first complete, I felt I was living in a blancmange. But I love this pink; fresh and cool in spring and summer; warm and cosy on winter evenings. Bright flashes of colour dart about the room: Marianna Kennedy's lamps, candles and coasters from my shop, and brightly coloured spines of the books in the bookcase that I built when I first moved in. The Hans Wegner Wishbone chair is the colour of Heinz Tomato Soup. I bought a pair, but that proved a little too much, and one migrated to my kitchen in Dorset, as you can see on pages 84–85.

DAVID HICKS
LIVING WITH DESIGN

PALLADIO
TOWN AND COUNTRY
The Last Country Houses
DESIGN OF CITIES
LEON BATTISTA ALBERTI
TUSCAN VILLAS
Baroque
FONTAINES
ITALIAN GARDENS
ITALIAN VILLAS AND PALACES
GREAT INTERIORS
ANDREA PALLADIO
NEW CLASSICISM
VENICE

LEFT Cool, and supremely elegant, just like its owner. This is my friend George Saumarez Smith's sitting room at his terraced house in Winchester. George designed the timber bookcases and the white painted timber fire surround, which carries a fine collection of Wedgwood Guyatt mugs. There is a modesty yet friendliness to this room that I love. Deep Howard armchairs sit comfortably either side of the woodburning stove; reading lamps are to hand just where they are needed; a contemporary white metal and glass table injects a sharper note, preventing this space from ever feeling dull and fusty.

ABOVE The sofa is made more comfortable still by George's collection of cushions, many bought at that excellent shop The Hambledon, in Winchester. A useful writing table is in the corner. The mustard yellow poster above picks up the colours of the cushions and the rug. But the space is dominated by Andrew Anderson's extraordinary linocut *The Rock of Cashel*, a mere corner of which appears in the photograph; one of the most remarkable works of art that I know. On the table in the foreground, an open copy of Anderson's book, *A Vision of Order*, printed and bound by The Whittington Press.

ABOVE A corner of Arne Maynard and William Collinson's sitting room at their house in Monmouthshire. A disparate collection of splendid pieces—elaborate wing chairs, a marble urn, a taxidermy rook—is arranged with the care of a curator's eye. Against the plain-boarded floor, whitewashed walls and leaded casements of the farmhouse, they have the lucid quality of a Flemish still life painting.

ABOVE LEFT The coastal retreat of a graphic designer and his wife. The images above demonstrate the transcendence of English taste. Both have white walls, and a sparse, restrained quality, yet one is composed predominantly with antiques, while this room has a wholly contemporary air. Hans Wegner chairs around a George Nelson table enjoy views onto a small courtyard garden. Note the model half-ships on the wall—almost abstract in their perfect form, and belonging to this seaside location.

LEFT High design need not be expensive. This cheery, lipstick red cabinet is from IKEA. But the collection of objects above reveals this to be the home of a collector. Appropriately for this distinguished graphic designer, they have the quality of blackface letters on a printed white page.

RIGHT All-encompassing comfort is offered by Arne Maynard and William Collinson's sofa. Kelim cushions and a blanket provide extra texture. A 'tablescape' beyond holds fragments of plaster, a Peter Hone bull plaque and a Marianna Kennedy resin lamp. I love the relationship between the soft pink freshly picked dahlias and the little oil painting adjacent.

ABOVE The West Dorset home of my friends Jason and Kate Goodwin. Wide rooms are filled with books and more books. This is one of my favourite houses, and one of the most comfortable I have ever been in. What delicious lunches have been eaten at this dining table, full of laughter and surrounded by the chaotic contentment of this happy family. The rooms are put together with the casual brilliance with which the Goodwins approach life. There is a warmth to the spines of old cloth-covered books that furnishes the simple spaces with no need for anything else.

RIGHT Is there anything more beautiful than this bright green corduroy chair? The Prussian blue velvet cushion adds a touch of glamour that transports us to the rich land of the Ottoman Empire, which provides the setting for Jason Goodwin's novels set in 1830s Istanbul.

FAR RIGHT A composition that takes on altogether surreal qualities. A bust of Homer presides over children's sculptures; a silk top hat dreams and speaks of glamorous dances. Geometric drawings by Jason Goodwin's father line the walls. What I find extraordinary about these photographs is that they were taken about a year after the Goodwins moved here, yet there is a settled quality that makes us feel we are in a room assembled over decades or more. Inspiration indeed!

OVERLEAF Architect Craig Hamilton and artist Diana Hulton's library at their home in the Welsh Borders: the comfort of knowledge. Hamilton designed these oak bookcases in 1997. The warm tones of the joinery and refectory table contrast with the cool stone-flagged floor.

Self-Sufficiency
TWELVE-TRIBE NATIONS
J.P. DONLEAVY
HELEN DUNMORE
watercolours
Musée d'Orsay The Guide to the Collections
THE BURRELL COLLECTION
PHILIP MANSEL

GILLOWS
GILLOWS
PALACES OF FLORENCE

THE ARCHITECTURE OF WREN

FRONT DR
STUDY
DINING RM
DRAWING RM
HALL
BACK DR
BEDROOMS
1
2
3
4
5

CHAPTER IV
Eating & Cooking

UPON A TALL, GENEROUS DRESSER is arranged, with care, a display of china: English delft and early Wedgwood, Richard Guyatt mugs, lustreware and charming Staffordshire figures. Placid light falls from a window overlooking the garden, casting a glow on the white-scrubbed beech kitchen table. Robust nineteenth-century fruitwood chairs, mismatched but related to one another, provide a comfortable spot to read the newspaper, make a shopping list or complete the crossword. Apricot walls and a red and black chequerboard quarry tiled floor warm the palette.

A dish of marrows brought in from the vegetable garden catches the light, a yellow courgette amongst them giving a flash of sharp acid relief to the quiet scene. All is still, as if waiting for the life of the house to burst in: the essence of an English kitchen, as if seen through the lens of Vermeer.

We are in one of my favourite kitchens, in a house in East Anglia designed in the 1930s that feels as if it has stepped out of a Ravilious watercolour. In my early architectural days, I made a detailed measured drawing of this dresser, a drawing that I still keep on file and ready for use today, for there is a quality of timelessness to its design that transcends decades; the timelessness that we find in all the best English rooms.

DICK TURPIN

CLIVE for
Huzza.
LANGOLEN
1
MILE

Grace darling

FOR DECADES, IF NOT CENTURIES, the reputation of English cooking left—how might one put it?—something to be desired. So all the more welcome is the revolution that has taken place in the last thirty years, which has seen such an extraordinary burgeoning of English artisan food producers, and interest in the food we eat and where it comes from. The place of eating and cooking within the home has never felt more important.

My kitchen in Dorset (see pages 84–85) is one of my favourite rooms in the world. Without wanting to resort to cliché, it really is the heart of the home. Once divided into two rooms, with a small, dark scullery that would in a previous generation have housed the maid, and a kitchen that had space only for cooking in, I removed a wall to create a generous, light-filled room in which everything—cooking, reading the papers, scrubbing potatoes, podding peas, flower arranging, writing emails, doing the laundry—happens around a long scrubbed table. Cool in the summer, and in winter the warmest room in the house, it is the place we all naturally gravitate to.

I think this must be true of all the best English kitchens. This chapter might have been titled 'Eating, Cooking & Living', were it not for the fact that I believe life should exist elsewhere, too. I am, after all, a subscriber to 'the Dining Room Preservation Society' (that is, to the magical alchemy of a dinner party by candlelight, when food, conversation, wine and atmosphere merge—in the enclosed, transformative, other-world of the Dining Room—to create a moment that, once in a while, feels outside of time itself). I admit to fearing for those houses where vast kitchens blur into giant living-television-and-games rooms. Where in this arena is the variety that makes life rich, or the privacy that makes it meaningful?

I also have something of a fear of over-fitted kitchens. I find that if you plan anything too carefully for the here and now, it will fall redundant sooner rather than later. This is as true of kitchens as it is of buildings. I prefer my kitchens to be like a handsome eighteenth-century townhouse—adaptable to changing needs and conditions, but not too carefully planned for any of them. I like a little old cupboard filled with spices and herbs, rather than a very organized drawer in which everything is cleverly and simultaneously on show. I have a particular loathing of fridges built in behind timber panelled doors...really? Occasionally, of course, something is so beautifully designed, and so carefully cherished over the decades, as to survive as a classic—the 1960s kitchen designed by the architect John Prizeman in David and Susan Gentleman's London house (see pages 92–93) being a wonderful case in point.

My approach to kitchen decoration, therefore, tends to rely on finding good old pieces of furniture that do the trick well: oak dressers with wide shelves or scrubbed pine tables with generous drawers. Built-in cupboards are sensible, and a practical way to maximize storage in a given width, but I would not plan them too carefully. When it comes to wire shelving that extends out of walls and hidden corners, I have a view that too many 'space-saving' devices seem to take up rather a lot of space in the end. There's a place in life for difficult-to-get-to backs of cupboards for the bits and pieces that you only need once a year.

Remember also that anything too clever has a tendency to disintegrate. My old kitchen at the Parsonage has a set of nineteenth-century cupboards—clearly cobbled together by an estate carpenter from a series of older doors—that are just as useful today as the day they were built. I am not sure that we will be saying the same of a perfectly fitted modern German kitchen 180 years from now. And we must acknowledge that one characteristic of English decoration is that, although it may never be quite right for the here and now, it is perfect forever.

PAGE 80 AND PREVIOUS PAGES It would be a marvellous thing to own one English delft plate; this carefully assembled collection is wonderful to behold, revealing the owners' particular interest in the period. My personal favourite can be found third from the right on the lower shelf; I have always had a great fondness for any sort of faux-marbling—so much nicer than the real thing.

RIGHT My own kitchen at The Old Parsonage, in West Dorset. Cupboards put together by an estate joiner in the nineteenth century are just as practical today as when they were built. My kind housekeeper polishes the brass knobs to a white gleam. On sunny days, the sunlight streams in through the window, which faces south across the valley. Here, cool, pale light falls gently across the grey painted floor. The armchair is just the sort of piece of furniture I like best: strong, simple and extremely comfortable.

Sel
FLOU

Three Classicists

ABOVE Lunch at The Old Parsonage: a loaf of bread, cheese, soup and a bowl of fruit. The dresser is both attractive and practical, home to dinner plates and green cabbage side plates. It is Welsh, eighteenth century, and people are sometimes a bit surprised (as was I) that I bought it on eBay. The kitchen clock was found a little more locally, in Dorchester, and bears the imprint of the maker. Orange candles from my shop and a bold Josef Frank fabric from Svenskt Tenn on the ball-back chairs give a jolt of colour to wake one up in the morning!

LEFT Looking across my kitchen in Dorset. I have never been a great fan of the fitted kitchen. So in this room, I am happy to make do with the tall range of cupboards seen to the right of the AGA, which contain everything from saucepans to groceries and spices. I bought the glass-fronted cabinet in a local junk shop, and added the timber cornice and a useful lower shelf. The dresser houses everything else, and just out of view behind the camera is a pair of stainless steel sinks, washing machine and dishwasher. A Sheila Maid laundry airer hangs above the AGA, warming clothes and linen quicker than one can imagine. As you can tell from these photographs, I've always been rather attracted to blue and white Victorian meat platters, which are still used whenever I roast a Sunday joint. The one hanging on the wall is a particularly nice Willow pattern, but is cracked—so is allowed into retirement.

1995

LEFT It would hardly be possible to conceive a more classic example of the English kitchen—although this gentle room is actually in a house in the Scottish borders designed by the architect Charles Morris. Everything is thoughtfully put together with an almost Edwardian concentration on detail and quality. Only the date plaque—set in the leaded stove back—reveals the year of construction to be 1995. Although probably not planned that way, everything has gravitated to the spot precisely where it is needed. A collection of small pots and omelette pans hangs above the stove. A wooden spice shelf has been installed to the right. A generous mantelshelf with beautifully designed brackets contains a collection of pottery and candlesticks. A hanging laundry-rack is the final touch, drying clothes above the warm AGA.

ABOVE To the same house, Charles Morris added a new wing in a perfectly balanced Arts and Crafts manner. The dining hall is a long, wide room lined with raised and fielded panelling painted a soft duck egg blue. The panelling stops 18 inches or so below the ceiling and a ledge cut in the uppermost moulding allows for the display of a collection of blue and white Chinese export porcelain. The dark oak furniture and reflective glass cabinet create a chiaroscuro range of tone in the pale room. To this, the owner has added the perfect note of contrast with a pink geranium in a clay pot. With its bright apple green leaves, it brings sparkling life to the entire harmonious ensemble.

RIGHT In the same room, a handsome oak side cupboard sits darkly, modestly below the shining frame of a southern landscape. The simple iron tie-back to the faded pink curtains demonstrates Charles Morris's attention to detail.

LEFT Could you imagine a cheerier kitchen than Peter Hone's blue on blue? Tucked into a tiny room in Peter's extraordinary, museum-like Notting Hill flat, his kitchen is one of the calmer and more restrained rooms in the house. Joyous eighteenth- and nineteenth-century china cups and jugs hang from the tiny dresser, mismatched but together creating a wonderful palette when one enjoys cups of China tea and rich chocolate éclairs at Peter's splendid table next door. A little gas stove, fridge and sink prove that we can be completely modest in our kitchen plans and still create one of the most beautiful rooms I know. Fish kettles and the *batterie de cuisine* hang from the wall above.

ABOVE Bright apple green walls add a note of freshness at Mrs Rosalind Ingrams' kitchen at Garsington Manor. This sunny room is in a service wing, added to the house in the 1920s. A dormer window above the door to the garden brings sunshine deep into the space. The kitchen table has fine Windsor chairs at either end, and plain nineteenth-century kitchen chairs around; piles of newspapers and books rest on the windowsill. An oiled kitchen tablecloth is practical, and archetypically English: buy Tana Lawn oilcloth from Liberty of London, or striped ticking oilcloth from Ian Mankin. Cork floor tiles are soft and warm underfoot, and are without doubt due a revival.

ABOVE Like a ship riding over a leaf green sea, the bay window of my dining room at The Old Parsonage is almost a little room in itself. The view faces south across to the gable of the church; the parson's gate from the garden into the churchyard is tucked under the buttress just visible in the photograph. In summer, I might have a small supper party at the table within the bay window. The table has been getting more and more wobbly—it really needs repair, but in the meantime I have tied up the legs, which does the trick for now. Broad curtains in cheap cotton ticking from Ian Mankin are perfect for children's amateur dramatics at Christmas.

RIGHT A view across the dining table. The chairs are William IV—which I think is probably my favourite period. They don't match, but are unified by brown Ian Mankin ticking seat covers. When I moved in, the builders stripped back buckets of glue from the floorboards. They wanted to stain and varnish them, but I forbade them from any further work. It's worth knowing when to stop. From time to time red wine stains appear, I cannot imagine how; but they add greatly to the charm of this floor. I love seagrass squares, which last really saw the light of day in the 1970s. Of all the things we have sourced in the shop, I am probably proudest of seagrass squares.

Salz.
BOSCH

LAWSON FOREVER SUMMER
NIGELLA LAWSON
HONEY FROM A WEED
Geographers' LONDON ATLAS
LONDON, W.
TUBOR FILTER

PREVIOUS PAGES The architect John Prizeman designed this serene kitchen in the 1960s. Now owned by David and Sue Gentleman, it has a timeless quality that sets it completely apart from most 'fitted' kitchens, which have a danger of dating as quickly as we change our socks. Why do I love this kitchen so much? It has an abstracted simplicity that is as relevant today as the day it was designed. But, more importantly, it combines perfectly with the old kitchen table, and cherrywood chairs, proving that this is not merely a period piece, but part of a living tradition of furniture and cabinet making. The glass milk bottles, needless to say, form a perfectly coordinating palette with the milky white tiles and upper cabinets.

ABOVE LEFT Another view of the Gentleman's kitchen, shown on the previous pages. The basement wall was knocked out to provide a light and leafy entrance courtyard. This was originally designed as a smaller kitchen with a separate, tiny dining room, but David and Sue Gentleman opened up the space to form a single, larger room with a generous kitchen table around which dinners and family parties take place. Light reflects around the room; you would not imagine you were in the basement of a nineteenth-century terraced house, originally the preserve of dark sculleries and coal stores.

BELOW LEFT AND FAR LEFT Two views of the open shelves of David and Sue Gentleman's kitchen: a simply arranged collection of practical kitchenalia that takes on a lucid, reverential quality owing to the care with which things are put together. A shelf of well-leafed cookbooks testifies to Susan Gentleman's delicious cooking, while the Victorian water filter has the graphic quality of an early David Gentleman book cover.

ABOVE A. N. Wilson and Ruth Guilding's dining room: a perfect room for long Sunday lunches where sparkling conversation flows as abundantly as food and wine. A plain mantelshelf displays a handsome collection of Wedgwood china. A. N. Wilson's father, Norman Wilson, designed for Wedgwood, becoming the firm's managing director, and many of these pieces are early prototypes. It was Wilson who recruited designers such as Ravilious, Bawden, Laura Knight, Keith Murray and Arnold Machin to the Wedgwood fold, creating a second golden age for the pottery to follow the great eighteenth-century achievements of Josiah Wedgwood. On the table, another Wedgwood mug, part of the splendid series of commemorative mugs designed by Richard Guyatt, contains a cheerful bunch of dahlias. Useful cupboards either side of the fireplace house plates and glasses.

MANHATTAN

LEFT My own kitchen in London. Over the years I've done a bit of work to this kitchen, most recently adding new cabinet doors to get rid of the hideous melamine cupboards that the rental flat came with. Oak or beech worktops from IKEA are a cheap and useful staple in such circumstances. The black and white lino floor provides a jaunty touch; I have long loved Josef Frank's 'Manhattan' fabric from Svenskt Tenn, which is perfect to use for a blind, and reminds me of my time in New York every day. I bought the aluminium Navy chair in New York, too, and it has lived in my various kitchens since.

ABOVE A few years ago I painted the kitchen walls this dark, sludgy brown-green colour from Farrow & Ball. It's a fantastic colour for a small kitchen, making the room warm and cosy, and providing a strong background against which to hang a collection of typographic prints and posters (including a pair of 'Tumbling Alphabets' by Hand & Eye Letterpress). I have always favoured open shelves rather than wall cupboards. They are not quite so practical, perhaps, for a London kitchen, but there's nothing nicer than a stack of plates on an open shelf. My father made the 'vine leaf' green dish when he was about ten years old, in Australia.

Marianna Kennedy and Charles Gledhill's kitchen at Fournier Street, Spitalfields: a classic early Georgian basement floor with plain panelled walls, to which Marianna and her collaborator James Howett have added a simple, continuous shelf on brackets running around the room. On the opposite wall, a Belfast sink and oiled teak draining board have an appropriately eighteenth-century character, and utensils and spices are all kept to hand. A stainless steel Smeg oven is the best-designed stove.

SALT
WHITE PEPPER
PAPRIKA

LEFT AND ABOVE George Saumarez Smith has made a large dining room and kitchen at his terraced house in Winchester, forming a new opening between the two rooms. The dining table is at the light-filled front of the house. The bold woven Basque linen tablecloth was a present from friends in New York. A set of mismatched chairs, collected over the years, make happy partners around the table. Edward Bawden's *Kew Palace* and Sheila Robinson's *Abingdon*, either side of the chimneybreast, are two of George's collection of mid-twentieth century linocuts. The mantelshelf holds commemorative mugs and pressed glass candlesticks, invitations and postcards. From the kitchen, double doors lead onto a balcony and stairs down to the garden.

RIGHT George Saumarez Smith designed his own plain, sturdy kitchen cabinets, reminiscent of a nineteenth-century butler's pantry. A contemporary note is added by the Bulthaup System 20 workbench. Originally designed with (presumably rather affluent) German students in mind, the workbench has become a design classic; sadly—like all the things I covet most—it is no longer in production. The contrast between its sleek stainless steel lines and the traditional cabinetry is particularly satisfying.

ABOVE A corner of Craig Hamilton and Diana Hulton's dining room. A set of three antique Greek glazed bowls rests on the side table; their yellow colour creates a subtle harmony with the tones of the dried flowers. A fragment of panelling, probably seventeenth-century Italian, hangs on the wall next to the doorway.

RIGHT Light falls gently on the uneven lime plaster walls; the oak framing and ceiling boards are limewashed, too, reflecting the light further around the room and creating a softly flaking palette of pale greys and whites. A collection of antique wine tureens is from Turkey and Spain; the pair of clay anthropomorphic effigy vessels is Mesoamerican. They have a happy presence in their deep niche. The linocut to the right is by John Muafangejo.

OVERLEAF Arne Maynard and William Collinson's kitchen in Monmouthshire: the timelessness of English decoration. This is a scene that has barely changed for centuries. The massive stone fireplace with rough-hewn surround has been limewashed white; an oversized log basket keeps the woodburning stove in fuel. I relish the way the light falls across the ancient stone flags; the broad kitchen table carries the simplest still life, of autumn fruits and burnt orange dahlias. Robust farmhouse chairs provide a comfortable place to sit. A generous antique cabinet with wide sliding doors is painted in the original soft blue-grey.

I WISH YOU WELL 3
GO WITH GOD
GO IN PEACE
I HOPE YOU WIllBECOME BACK
TO US ONE DAY

TEA

ENGLISH DOWNLAND
DICK FRANCIS
DICK FRANCIS ENQUIRY

CHAPTER V
A Quiet Retreat

AND WHEN ALL IS DONE, it is time to rest, and to restore, and to envelop ourselves in the quiet comforts of bedroom and bathroom. I sometimes think we feel the spirit of a house most strongly in these rooms. A sense of retreat and withdrawal from the day-to-day is implicit. Just as an ancient house settles at night, creaking softly in the cooling night air, so do we lie down, stretch, rest and prepare for the new day.

Here are the private places, the rooms where we fall asleep, or wake to dawn's first soft grey light, or bathe and change before dinner, as the golden rays of sunset stream in through open windows, while 'westering, questioning settles the sun', in Betjeman's lyrical words.

My own bedroom, in Dorset, has a long view down the Bride Valley that, were it not for an ancient clump of trees, would look far down to the sea at West Bay. From the opposite window, I see into the branches of the old copper beech that grows next to the house, which during winter storms sounds as if about to fall into the room itself. In spring, the leaves unfold with vivid claret red that slowly dissolves to the ink-blackness of midsummer, by which time it feels as if I sleep in a treehouse. At night it is silent apart from the calls of owls, and completely dark save for the light of stars or the moon.

WHAT MAKES THE perfect bedroom? Proportions of the room are important—extraordinarily, but truly, I find I sleep best in a room that is not too large. How is it that we can sense the volume of a room in the pitch dark? I have never known, but I think we can tell. And for this the dimensions must relate to the size of the house. A bedroom at my parsonage, perfectly cosy and snug, would feel mean spirited and cramped in a far grander house, and far too palatial in a cottage.

In an age of central heating, fireplaces are rarely lit; but is there anything nicer than staying with friends in the country who still, on a winter's evening, light fires in their guest rooms? No, there is not—except, that is, to be woken the following morning with a cup of tea, and the sound of the fire being revived, and curtains being pulled back to reveal the flat grey light of a February morning. I love the warmth of the morning bed linen in contrast to the chill air of waking in an old English house in the middle of winter.

In summer, I like to wake early—with the dawn; the extraordinary morning chorus reaching its deafening peak on May mornings, where in our wooded valley the sound of birdsong becomes overwhelming. Nothing makes me happier than waking, savouring the potential of the day, while the rest of the house is asleep; or, likewise, of being about in London before the world wakes up and begins its cacophonic symphony. Gone, I suppose, are the days of Nancy Mitford, who would spend the entire morning lying in bed corresponding—although one wonders if the Blackberry and laptop are our latter-day response?

A bed should have soft sheets and deep pillows. My personal favourite is Olatz linen from New York, but in the country I prefer plain white cotton. My housekeeper Anne irons everything to a taut smoothness and makes up the beds so that the sheets are like a slab of white marble. Beds should be bordered by comfortable reading lights, on nightstands that are generous enough to house books, magazines and a water glass and jug. For insomniacs like me, a block of notepaper and box of pencils are essential ingredients, together with a Roberts radio by the bed—to connect one to other sleepless people listening to the news from around the world at 3.30am.

Chairs and sofas are less for sitting in than for scattering clothes over at night. Some prefer the comfort of a soft wool carpet underfoot, in which case select a plain, neutral weave in a flat, subdued colour (French grey would be my personal choice). I have always preferred seagrass or jute, overlaid with rugs and kelims in faded colours. Chests of drawers and wardrobes are easily found in borrowed corners from home, or can be picked up for a song at local weekly auctions: choose unadorned eighteenth- and nineteenth-century mahogany or oak or, in the country, old painted pine; I loathe fitted cupboards unless they are very carefully designed and made to have all the substance of a proper piece of country house joinery.

Bedrooms are often most beautiful when wallpapered. Otherwise, they should be painted in calm shades of off-white and grey; although I am thinking about painting my tiny bedroom in London a rich, dark colour so that it is a snug cocoon at night. Soft chintzes, small-patterned fabrics and warm-coloured textiles make us feel at home. I love sleeping in a room with fabric-lined walls and the stillness, the comfort, that that offers.

No one need mourn the loss of the chilly English bathroom; we have Nancy Lancaster to thank for bringing this once fearful space into the realm of civilization. Deep bathtubs, in which one may take a lingering soak, generous washstands, piles of towels, magazines and flowers extend the language of the bedroom into the bathroom, banishing the cold linoleum and sanatorium chinaware of a previous generation once and for all, and for the good.

PAGE 106 AND PREVIOUS PAGES My bedroom at The Old Parsonage. This room looks out onto a leafy scene and in the height of summer takes on a soft green hue that is at once calm and fresh. The curtain fabric is a twig pattern by Colefax and Fowler, one of that venerable fabric house's classic small prints that tragically have been discontinued. The floorcovering is seagrass, with a faded kelim rug. The Victorian fruitwood chairs have Gothick pattern, at home with the village church opposite. On the mantelpiece are Edward VIII and George VI coronation mugs, by Ravilious for Wedgwood.

RIGHT A top floor bedroom of a village house in Essex. A 1930s Heal's brass bed sits comfortably beside a fine Georgian desk and writing chair. The pink and lilac of the patchwork quilt sing beautifully against the pale apricot walls. A tiny moulding and shelf makes for a simple but extremely elegant fire surround.

ABOVE AND ABOVE RIGHT Two views of the stair and landing at Iain and Zara Milligan's house in Scotland. A small window, with operating shutters within the deep wall reveals, lights a superb early portrait; the handsome painted timber staircase has unusual flat balusters and gentle round newel posts designed by Charles Morris. The sloping ceilings of the landing (above right) belong to the older part of the house.

RIGHT A small guest bedroom in the same house has been lined with painted beaded board to make it as snug as the cabin of a little ship. Polished mahogany furniture and a lamp, books, china and a scattering of framed prints and engravings add a modestly luxurious touch to an otherwise small and undistinguished room.

LEFT Glimpsed from the landing in the pictures above, the small bedroom at Iain and Zara Milligan's house. This is one of two guest bedrooms in the tower house designed by Charles Morris. A warm-toned Zoffany wallpaper is both pretty and cosy; a generous chest of drawers bears a tall lamp with a green marbled paper lampshade. A richly coloured Persian rug and a delicate printed and embroidered bedspread complete the layers of pattern. It is hard to imagine that this beautiful room is less than twenty years old.

ABOVE LEFT AND RIGHT The extraordinary guest bedroom at Garsington, the home of Mrs Rosalind Ingrams. The wallpaper is of Italian design, and was installed when the house was used in the 1995 film *Carrington*. In the 1920s, Garsington was the home of Philip and Lady Ottoline Morrell, and became famous as a centre of the Bloomsbury Group: Aldous Huxley, T. S. Elliot, D. H. Lawrence, Mark Gertler, Dora Carrington and Lytton Strachey all came to stay here. The turquoise blue ground and elaborate ruby red, gold and green pattern responds perfectly to the Ingrams' beautiful and ancient Italian beds, two of which, curiously, are housed in this room.

RIGHT Another bedroom at Garsington has a vivid blue block-printed wallpaper, a palette enriched by the duck egg blue panelling picked out in cerulean. The fruitwood tones of the bed and the delicate, fragile late eighteenth-century box piano are warm against the marine palette. The grey marble fireplace dates to the 1720s, a near identical cousin to the one in my own sitting room in London, shown on page 69.

LEFT A plain, deep ultramarine mochaware mug, with finely turned base and perfectly formed handle. Mochaware—that most handsome of nineteenth-century pottery styles—makes a recurring appearance through this book; it is fascinating to see how many of my friendships are united by collections of mochaware mugs and jugs!

LEFT This guest bedroom at a house in Suffolk is country house style at its best. A splendid nineteenth-century dolls house sits in front of a mahogany door with a crisp, white painted architrave. The wallpaper ground is a magical cornflower blue, overprinted with a French pattern of stars and wreaths. To the right of the mahogany coat stand is a blue-grey velvet Coronation chair. These chairs were given to all those who attended the 1937 Coronation of King George VI and Queen Elizabeth. Its austere lines, pale gilt braiding and embroidered insignia belong to that same moment as the Ravilious Coronation mugs on my bedroom mantelshelf, shown on pages 108–109.

ABOVE A bedroom landing at Garsington Manor. Three disparate chests of drawers have migrated, as if in conversation with one another, to this friendly spot on the wide, ancient landing; in the foreground, an Anglo-Indian piece, inlaid with mother of pearl, and then plain examples of Georgian mahogany. The nonchalant way in which they are juxtaposed is characteristic of the relaxed atmosphere of this magical house. There is a great deal of Englishness in such relaxation. Piles of books and linen wait (perhaps for years?) to move elsewhere. A marvellous giant-scaled block-printed wallpaper unites the space.

ABOVE The guest bathroom at George Saumarez Smith's house in Winchester. Tiled in chartreuse yellow, with handmade tiles from Emery et Cie, and with an oversized showerhead from Lefroy Brooks, this is a splendid room in which to take a morning bath. George designed the teak bath surround and panelling.

ABOVE LEFT AND LEFT George Saumarez Smith's guest bedroom continues a similar chartreuse green colour theme in the small velvet-covered slipper chair and in the lining to the fireplace. A printed cotton bedspread, and cushions bought from Anokhi in New Delhi, add a touch of soft colour. Linocuts by Sheila Robinson hang on the walls.

RIGHT A corner of George's own bedroom, A grey linen armchair has a cushion from Thornback & Peel; the bright green printed cotton bedspread is from Country & Eastern in Norwich. A cream bedside lamp on the little mahogany bookcase has a 1930s feel, and a small bunch of narcissi are in a beautiful seagreen mochaware mug. Hanging on the walls is part of George's collection of printed linocuts; the picture on the left is by renowned printmaker Angie Lewin, and shows the same George VI coronation mug as you might see on my bedroom mantelshelf (pages 108–109). The rug in the foreground, perfect in colour and composition, was designed by George's grandfather, the distinguished architect Raymond Erith, and hand cross-stitched by his grandmother, Pamela.

EMILY EDEN
Two Novels
SIR ROBERT TAYLOR
MARCUS BINNEY
GREEK AND ROMAN ARCHITECTURE
HAMLIN
Greek Revival Architecture in America
GREEK ARCHITECTURE
Southill: a Regency House

THIS PAGE Peaceful, modest simplicity in David and Sue Gentleman's London bedroom. A low, plain bed with a white cotton spread, simple tables from IKEA and a pair of anglepoise lamps are all that adorns this luminous, timeless room. But it needs no decoration; tall sash windows overlook a leafy street, the verdant richness of the exterior brought inside by the tree that grows between them. The connecting bathroom–dressing room, left, is lined with tall cupboards wallpapered in William Morris's 'Willow Boughs'. This is a green and leafy eyrie; one of the calmest and most English rooms I know.

ABOVE Marianna Kennedy and Charles Gledhill's bedroom at 3 Fournier Street, Spitalfields: an early eighteenth-century room given a contemporary twist. A four-poster bed has a soft yellow bedcover, matched in the yellow bookcloth blinds (which Marianna sells from her shop downstairs). In the windows, lattice privacy screens filter the light; the noise and bustle of East London can be completely shut out at night by closing the wooden shutters. Classical prints complete the monochromatic palette; the final flourish is provided by one of Marianna's enigmatic paintings from her 'Dites-Moi' series.

ISLE OF WIGHT
OLD TOWNS REVISITED

LEFT AND ABOVE The attic bedroom at The Old Parsonage. When I moved to the house, this low attic bedroom was forlorn, damp and a little unloved. I designed a wall of beaded-board panelling to cover a curiously projecting chimneybreast, and to lend to the room the feeling of being in a small cabin or treehouse. From the tiny dormer windows there is an extraordinary view across our deeply wooded valley. A pair of Victorian hospital beds came from the magnificent depository at Wessex Beds in Somerset. Each has block-printed Indian bedcovers, and duck egg blue Welsh blankets by my friend Eleanor Pritchard, which we sell in my shop. A geological map of the Isle of Wight, where my parents live, hangs above the small oak chest of drawers. A ledged door leads to a tiny landing that over the years has become home to a rather strange collection of taxidermy. This bedroom tends to be slept in by friends' children, and a small, ancient rocking horse sits in the corner to keep them company at night.

ABOVE In Arne Maynard and William Collinson's house in Monmouthshire, a guest bedroom not just to sleep in. Can you imagine any nicer place to be laid up for weeks, slowly working one's way through these tantalizing bookshelves? I love books in a bedroom. These generous shelves, built in beneath a substantial timber beam, take that rule to an extreme, but a worthy one. The low ceiling, walls the soft brown-pink colour of mushroom gills and the beautifully made patchwork quilt create an air of contented cosiness that would be hard to better. Yet the bed is tucked up against the leaded casement window; a perfect place to wake early on a summer's morning. A magnificent carved oak chair and watchful cardinal add a spirit of grandeur to a farmhouse interior.

LEFT In the same house, the master bedroom has an entirely different scale. Massive Welsh oak beams rise to the ceiling; a huge oak lintel above the fireplace testifies to the substantial, timeless solidity with which such houses were built. The plain whitewashed walls and ancient, wide plank oak floors have a monastic simplicity. This room would surely still be recognized by the people who built it. Arne Maynard and William Collinson have not sought to soften this grandeur, but instead to work in harmony with it. A broad, dark oak chest is by the door; fire irons are ready to tend to a blazing log fire in the depths of the Welsh winter. A pair of ancient rugs adds warmth; the generous bed is humble to the architecture of the space as a whole.

ABOVE In David and Sue Gentleman's Suffolk cottage, the first floor bedrooms lead one to another, in the manner of many old country buildings. Far from subdividing the rooms, the Gentlemen have celebrated the convivial domesticity that arises. In the main bedroom, walls of butter yellow are sparsely decorated with simple pictures; my favourite of the famous School Prints series, John Nash's *Harvesting*, hangs between the open doors. The balusters of the stair are echoed in the open timber studwork above.

RIGHT Looking back, a simple cast-iron bedstead dominates this child's room. Light from the window bounces off the crisp, white bedlinen; a small patterned wallpaper in pink and blue decorates one wall, and unusual curtains with playful kittens in a tree pick up the same theme. A little cotton rag rug softens the step; remarkably wide plank floors lend a generous scale, and a tiny seagull model is ever in flight, to keep young occupants of this bed in happy and untroubled dreams.

ABOVE These two bathrooms, in an Essex house, were designed in the 1930s by a young classical architect and have not been changed since. They have a lucid simplicity and dignity. The arched, marble-lined recesses that house the plain, cast-iron bathtubs have something of the character of that great English nineteenth-century architect Sir John Soane. In this blue bathroom, a playful white painted chair and cheery checked bathmat lighten the tone.

LEFT Looking into the yellow bathroom, one is struck by the elegant curves of the fruitwood caned nursing chair, upholstered in a pretty fabric from Zoffany. White towels (the only colour to have) warm on a chunky nickel-plated towel rail; a shaggy bathmat is soft underfoot: simple but generous luxuries. The sky blue canister is Portmeirion. I love the plain simplicity with which the soap niche is formed. The bathtub is fronted with an elegant single slab of grey Carrara marble.

ABOVE A plain, nicked-framed mirror in the blue bathroom reflects the arched niche in which the bathtub lies. A spare, elegant timber shelf holds a single nineteenth-century Spode lidded dish. There is a restraint, a lack of show, in this detail that speaks eloquently of the 1930s and the stripped-back language of design in this period, which makes Edwardian (and many contemporary bathrooms) appear fussy by comparison. Note the subtle way in which the clean marble edge of the bath niche is finished flush with the perfectly finished plaster walls.

ABOVE A little mahogany stand in my own bathroom, at home in Dorset. I love this piece of furniture for its plainness yet its grace, the simple turned corner posts in the form of Doric columns. It makes a good place for books and magazines, and for white geranium plants in clay pots. The bathtub is completely plain, with the cheapest white 6-inch square tiles around the wall, and chrome taps from Barber Wilsons which, I think, make the most robust of the traditional designs.

RIGHT The guest bathroom at The Old Parsonage. Here, the walls and bath are lined in painted beaded board, with a useful shelf for people to put their bits and pieces on while they are staying. A delicate Regency bamboo chair is a good spot to sit, or for towels. The red and grey striped runner is a leftover from carpeting my staircase.

ABOVE LEFT AND LEFT At Iain and Zara Milligan's house in Scotland, Charles Morris designed this guest bathroom lined entirely in painted beaded board. The washstand and bath surround are of black slate, and the long-spout taps are polished nickel, creating a mood of restrained comfort. Engravings are hung against the panelled walls. The window is small, so Charles devised a simple iron swing-rail for the curtain, which folds shut when privacy is required. When it is not, there is a lovely view up the drive from this window, best seen while enjoying a steaming soak in the extremely long bathtub.

ABOVE A tiny niche in the same bathroom is built in around a sloping chimneybreast. Ultramarine paint provides a splash of vivid colour behind a collection of shells and other fragments. A Victorian fruitwood towel rail has a particularly attractive profile and carries a warm brown towel, the colour of which matches the dark chocolate joinery.

LEFT Arne Maynard and William Collinson's guest bathroom, with robust, lapped oak boarding forming a natural, warmly panelled room that feels both historic and contemporary. This character is maintained with the use of a simple, utilitarian washbasin and taps. Similar examples can be found either from architectural salvage merchants or from suppliers of chinaware for industrial use. We all look better bathing by candlelight, and the wrought-iron sconces with thick church candles cast a warm, flickering light in the evening. Touches of comfort are offered by the Persian rug on the floor, by a pleasantly leaning towel rail and by the freshly picked flowers on the deep windowsill.

ABOVE LEFT In the same house, the master bathroom is lined with beaded-board panelling to dado height, with a deep shelf for water glasses and toothbrush mugs, a Victorian mahogany mirror and a changing display of seedheads from the garden, found objects and framed photographs. There is simplicity yet richness here. The dark chocolate paint is a strong choice, contrasting beautifully with the whitewashed walls. The wide floorboards are painted in off-white gloss paint, a practical surface for a country bathroom. Note how the Victorian clawfoot bathtub and china washbasin are propped on timber wedges, keeping things level on the dramatically sloping floor.

Radiant sunshine streams in through the Georgian sash window of Marianna Kennedy's London bathroom. Filtered by an elegant timber lattice screen, by a soft pink bookcloth blind, and then by the simple cotton towel on a slender ancient rail, the light glows against the polished plaster walls and splashes onto a pair of ebonized Regency Gothick cane chairs. This is a luxurious room, with its deep, cast-iron bath, simple china basin and handsome nickel taps. But the magic touch is provided by the deep red lacquered frame, which at once wakes the space and tells us that we are not in the preserve of a Neo-Georgian fogey, but instead that of one of London's most brilliantly stylish flames.

A present for Papa

CHAPTER VI
Rooms of Utility

SIMPLE SHELVES ON STURDY BRACKETS, stacked with crockery; thick gloss paint on walls and joinery; ancient brick, tile or stone-flagged floors, worn in undulating patterns by years of use; elsewhere, off bedroom landings, rooms lined with deep mahogany cupboards containing piles of folded linens, sheets and blankets.

These are the ingredients of Rooms of Utility. If they lack the grandeur and fireworks that we find elsewhere in English rooms, they are all the more special and thoughtful for it. Nothing here is superfluous; everything has purpose, and is designed for the task to hand. Decoration is notable for its absence—these are rooms not thought about, designed or considered in anything other than a practical sense.

And yet—why is it that these are always our favourite rooms in the house? Because a lingering part of us prefers the dignity of utility to the empty frivolity of gilt; we flock to the simple rooms and servants' halls of great houses rather than to drawing rooms thick with Aubusson carpets and heavy with French furniture. Not just, I think, because we find more of ourselves in the humble spaces than the grand. It is that in their very essence we find a truth; and the honesty of these good, plain, below-stairs places is always more appealing than charade.

A FEELING OF CALM RESONATES, quietly, from the house where everything finds its place. I love that sense of inevitability, of decorum, that arises in what we might call the 'well-tempered' home.

Extensive and generous rooms of utility are too often forgotten in today's homes, yet they give space for the rest of the house to breathe. When I am designing a house, I always force myself to remember—again and again—those spaces for boots and coats, for laundry and linen, for larders and pantries and sculleries; cellars for wine and winter vegetables; attics for storage and for old furniture. It is true that they are never quite as exciting to draw as panelled dining rooms and lofty staircases, or elaborate columned halls; but in their way they are all the more important. We cannot have the one without the other.

My tiny flat in London is a mere 350 square feet (about 32.5 square metres). Why is it such a pleasure to live there? Not just because of the marble fireplace and panelled rooms earlier. It is also because of the walk-in cupboard that contains everything from ironing board and spare kitchenalia to stepladders and toolbox; and another generous clothes cupboard, which last year I had lined in cedar. The architect who converted the flat in the 1970s did a thoughtful job. Even in this tiny space, he considered the hidden spaces as much as the rooms themselves.

The photographs in these pages have a calm, a stillness, in which we can find poetry. These are the quiet spaces, where a plate of vegetables set on a black slate shelf in the larder takes on the power of a still life by William Nicholson or the Delft school, or a hallway has the intensity of a watercolour by Eric Ravilious. In others, lost corners of a grander country house, the sense of order gives way to a magical, Aladdin's cave-like quality, where we can only anticipate what treasures might be resting amongst the heaving shelves of china and glass.

Floors should be practical: brick, stone, quarry tile, linoleum, scrubbed boards. In these rooms they need to be mopped and scrubbed. Walls are plain white, or blue, or bold acid yellow to banish the gloom of a London basement. Joinery is gloss white, or a strong apple green. Lighting is utilitarian but practical, with metal or glass shades providing bright illumination just where it is needed for the task in hand. Furniture is old; perhaps migrating from smarter rooms: tin-topped tables, slate or marble slabs that may be wiped clean, and which stay cool in the heat. Everything has purpose, but from purpose, with care, we may still achieve a sense of display: copper pans on a shelf, baskets and seed boxes in a garden hallway.

Some rooms of utility take on a different character. These are the offices, rooms of work but not of storage or of household management; they are rooms of makers, and artists. One of my favourite rooms of all—sadly dismantled before I was writing this book—was the attic office of the architect Charles Morris, in his rambling Elizabethan house in Suffolk. An old wooden desk, a plan chest, olive green filing cabinets and Charles's tiny drawing board; all where it was needed. A Georgian hob grate kept the room warm in chilly East Anglian winters. From a tiny dormer window he could look down across an ancient riverine landscape, in those flat fields where Norfolk meets Suffolk.

I find no places more beautiful than these: consider here the studio of the artist David Gentleman, or of Spitalfields bookbinder Charles Gledhill, suffused in a brilliant late autumn afternoon glow. Everything is devoted to a purposeful and practical end. These rooms take on their own beauty; who is to argue that Gentleman's carefully arranged rulers and set squares, pencils and brushes have not their own form of intense, totemic intent? Everything is to hand, exactly where it is needed, never lost, and finding the beauty that arrives from utility itself.

PAGE 136 AND PREVIOUS PAGES Country house joinery at its best: the beautiful, apple green cupboards in Mrs Rosalind Ingrams' pantry at Garsington. An old Roberts radio, a ubiquitous ingredient of every English house, sits alongside useful teapots and jugs. In the china cabinet, piles of crockery and meat platters are to hand for every eventuality.

RIGHT The startling, chrome yellow gloss-painted walls of Ruth Guilding and A. N. Wilson's basement, showing the stone-flagged hallway leading to the garden. Although this is a dark space, any sense of gloominess is banished by this fantastic colour; light literally bounces around the room. An old dresser is painted gloss white and is home to a display of 'Persephone' plates by Ravilious for Wedgwood. The stairs are formed of thick Yorkstone slabs with single iron balusters let into each tread.

LEFT David and Sue Gentleman's boot room at their Suffolk cottage. Nothing in this scene jars the eye. A wide boarded and ledged door leads into a room that is at once entirely practical and absolutely beautiful. Particularly special is the old 'gault' brick floor. Gault bricks, made of a white clay, are characteristic of East Anglia, but hard to find today; check reclamation yards and websites. They must be laid tight butt-jointed, never with a cement grout. Over time, like these, the bricks will become polished by use to a pale, reflective surface; minor impurities in the clay shine more brightly. Against the wall, a row of wellington boots stand waiting for walks, and a low bentwood chair helps when pulling them on and off. An enamel bucket sits by the old bread oven.

ABOVE Perfect simplicity in the larder at Garsington Manor: plain white walls and shelves on brackets; thick grey slate shelves to keep food cool; bowls and baskets, empty jars awaiting jams and marmalade, and rows of green bottles for next year's elderflower cordial. Why is it that in this practical room we can also find great beauty? It is partly due to the sense of quiet, harmonious good order that we sense at work. And it is partly, too, the sense of timelessness that gives this picture the quality of a still life painting—look at the way that light softly touches the walls and shelves. But, above all, the beauty stems from restrained simplicity, whereby nothing has been thought about too much; it just is as it is. When designing a new house, this sense of inevitability is the hardest thing of all to achieve.

LEFT At a manor house in Suffolk, this useful room leads directly off a warm, sunny kitchen. Contrasting with the white walls, all the joinery is painted a soft, warm grey—Farrow & Ball's Hardwick White would be a similar choice. A dog basket has a snug home within the old chimneybreast; coffee pots and jars reveal a family who take simple pleasures carefully. Above the fireplace is a handsome old advertising mirror from a Victorian pub. Shelves are lined with cookbooks. Below sits an essential piece of survival kit in the English country house: a supplementary heater. In rambling old houses, the central heating system is never quite enough to deal with cold snaps. To have things otherwise would not, really, be English, although we have moved on a little from the days when it was useful to have a dog on the bed in the middle of winter to keep you warm while you slept.

RIGHT Mrs Ingrams' scullery at Garsington: to my mind, one of the most beautiful rooms in this book. Pale blue walls (the colour, historically, was thought to discourage flies) are clean and fresh against bright white joinery, a deep Belfast sink and the old Victorian painted table with its piles of newspapers destined for recycling. Pots and pans, baskets and bins line every shelf. There is nothing else to it: no more, no less; yet again, for me, this is a space as pure and as reverential in its way as a tiny side chapel that you might find in an ancient Tuscan church.

RIGHT Tucked in below a sloping roof in a tiny outshot, Zara Milligan's scullery has plain cupboards and a massive Belfast sink, designed by architect Charles Morris. Charles placed this little window to bring light and a sense of space to the room; can you think of a nicer place to prepare the dog food and do a bit of washing-up? Teak countertops are warm and forgiving. The taps have their own personality; the rubber nozzle is another ubiquitous piece of English kit, which the practical housewife will not be without. A little line and clothes-pegs make a useful way to write memos, not unlike the serving line of a busy restaurant!

BREA

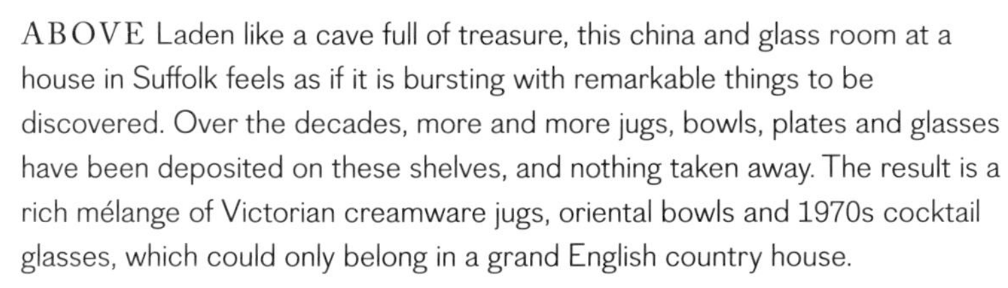

ABOVE Laden like a cave full of treasure, this china and glass room at a house in Suffolk feels as if it is bursting with remarkable things to be discovered. Over the decades, more and more jugs, bowls, plates and glasses have been deposited on these shelves, and nothing taken away. The result is a rich mélange of Victorian creamware jugs, oriental bowls and 1970s cocktail glasses, which could only belong in a grand English country house.

LEFT The scullery that leads off the kitchen on pages 78 and 80–81; effectively the working half of the same room. The architect designed these simple, perfectly proportioned and detailed cupboards, with an oiled teak worktop that drains to a broad white china sink. The brass cabinet knobs are particularly nice. Little chrome taps are fed by gleaming copper pipes, kept polished on a weekly basis. The plainest white tiles have a clean and handsome appearance. The shelves above contain rows of aluminium pans, colanders and implements, each one in its place. A small milk-glass shade hangs above the sink; the same black and red quarry tiles and apricot-coloured walls unite the room with the kitchen next door.

RIGHT At Zara Milligan's pantry in Scotland, shelves are again tucked into the low sloping eaves of a small outshot at the back of the house. No space is wasted, and there is a fine display of preserves and liqueurs, olive oils, champagne and mixers. I get as much pleasure in looking at such a generously stocked set of shelves as visiting The National Gallery.

ABOVE A polar opposite to the beautiful disorder of Suffolk (above left), William Collinson's jars of marmalades and preserves, at his and Arne Maynard's house in Monmouthshire, are as precisely ordered as a regiment on display. Lined up in neat rows on an old Georgian oak shelf, they demonstrate the quiet sense of pleasure that derives from the well-tempered home—and speak of sufficiency, and useful presents for friends. I love the stacked egg boxes, ready for gathering eggs and chitting potatoes in the spring.

LEFT Arne Maynard and William Collinson's boot room in Monmouthshire has the quality of an ancient tomb or castle. The lofty ceiling and top lighting emphasize the extraordinary pattern and texture of the rubble stone wall and floor; an ancient oak chest has a bone-dry quality, and antlers lend a baronial air. Rows of boots and wellingtons lie ready for working in the garden or for walks.

FAR LEFT The tack room in this house in Suffolk gives us the feeling of having walked into the burial chamber of an ancient Egyptian pyramid, or the storerooms of a beautiful museum, as if we are encountering this space for the first time in centuries. A fine layer of white dust lies gently across every surface; some of these saddles and riding hats have not been moved for decades. Victorian china and 1920s seltzer bottles jostle for space alongside a collection of ancient wire coat hangers. The whole still life sits against a backdrop of intense Prussian blue walls. I am reminded here of the back offices at Calke Abbey.

LEFT A small outhouse at David and Sue Gentleman's Suffolk cottage contains a lovely and varied collection of Victorian china, quietly arranged with space between each vase, each ready to receive a generous bunch of cow parsley, or daffodils or, in the autumn, dahlias. I am a great believer in such a collection of vases and jars. Nice plain china like this can still be picked up in street markets everywhere for next to nothing. I would rather have one friendly vase like this than an entire cabinet of cut-glass Waterford crystal.

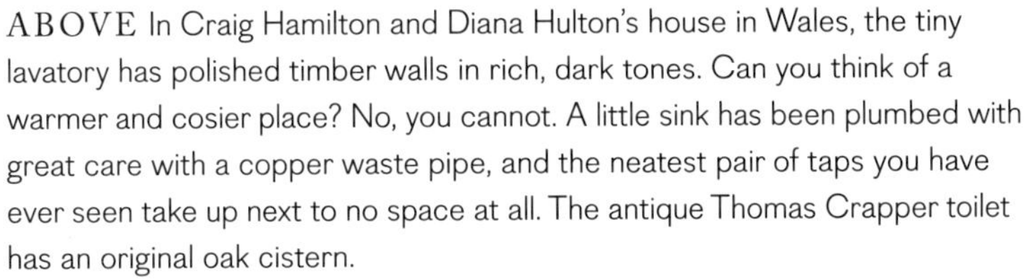

ABOVE In Craig Hamilton and Diana Hulton's house in Wales, the tiny lavatory has polished timber walls in rich, dark tones. Can you think of a warmer and cosier place? No, you cannot. A little sink has been plumbed with great care with a copper waste pipe, and the neatest pair of taps you have ever seen take up next to no space at all. The antique Thomas Crapper toilet has an original oak cistern.

LEFT The country house lavatory is most frequently referred to, in the country, as the 'gents', and this room has as an appropriately masculine air. The doors are painted to look like mahogany. The walls are white and hung with old maps in frames; the floor is made of old pamments. Glimpsed through the open door is the hallway, lined with drawings by the distinguished architect owner, and hung with paper to look like stone. It is interesting to note that there is nothing wrong with surface-mounted pipework, so long as it is neatly done; things like plumbing need not be hidden or boxed away.

ABOVE At Garsington Manor, the downstairs lavatory is a generous, sunny room, in which one is tempted to linger. A charming Pugin wallpaper and William Morris linen curtains lend the room an air of a nineteenth-century vicar's study, were it not for the basin and lavatory tucked around the corner. Piles of books and magazines (including *The Oldie*, edited by Rosalind Ingrams' brother-in-law, Richard) add to the temptation to take rather too long in the room.

OVERLEAF This little study in a corner of David and Sue Gentleman's Suffolk cottage has a quiet, pared-down charm. An ancient map of the coast hangs on the whitewashed wall and catches the light, as if painted by a Dutch master. Gardening books line the shelves above the fruitwood chair and desk; David's easels and painting boxes are to one side, and his set squares and draughting tools hang by the leaded light window. Baskets contain tennis rackets and balls; a jug of old-fashioned English roses sits on the windowsill. This is the sort of room we all need.

THE GARDENING YEAR
FLORA BRITANNICA
RICHARD MABEY
ALDRINGHAM WITH THORPE
SUDBOURNE
CHILLESFORD
ORFORD

DG's books:
good printed proof sheets
Wood engraving proofs
and DG greetings cards
Book jackets and
paperback covers
Journals, calendars
and other ephemera
Early RCA work and
printed work by Dad
OIL PAINTING
SONY
HEALEYS PRINT GROUP

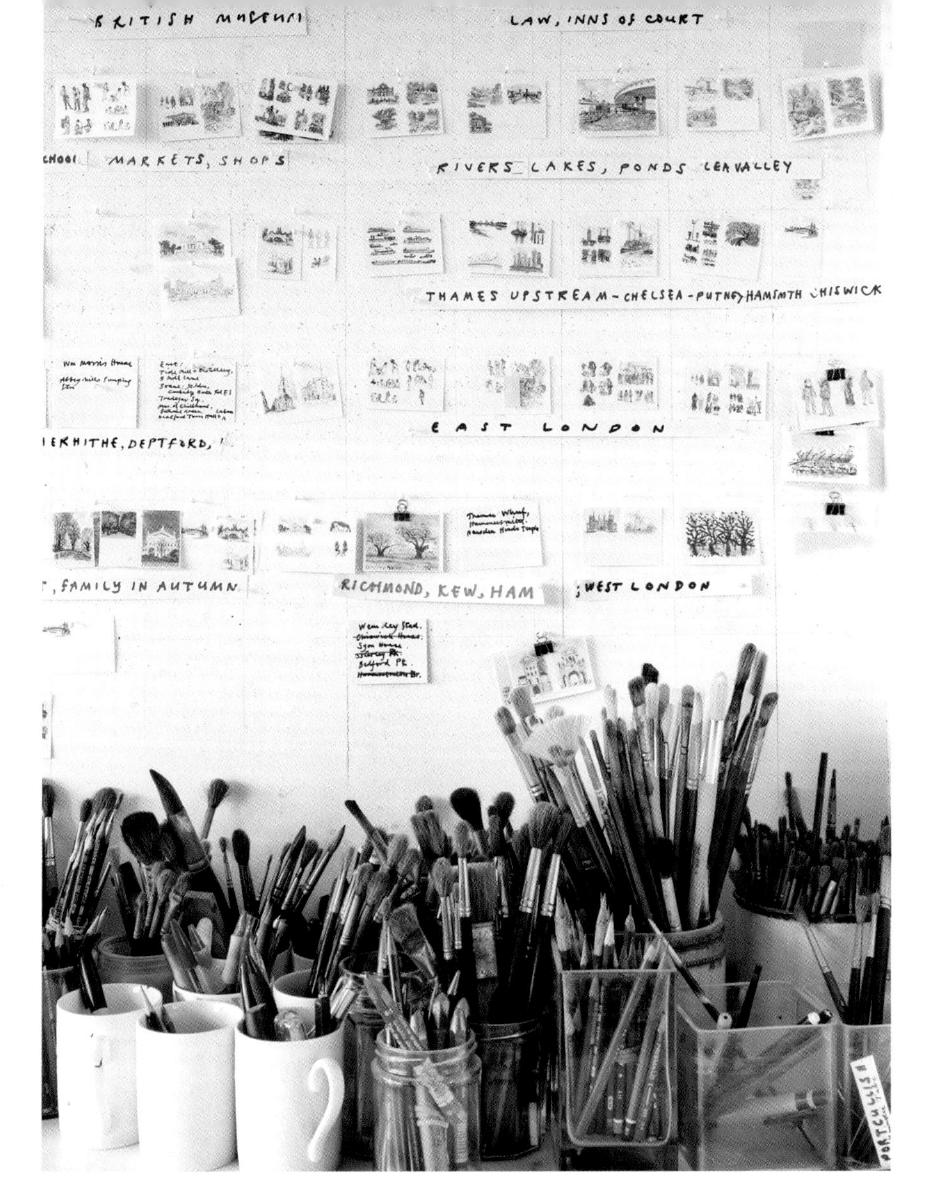

FAR LEFT A corner of David Gentleman's studio on the top floor of a Regency house in Camden. Rooms of utility need not be just for storage or laundry, but for any place of work. This view looks through from the studio to the stair landing, with its plan chest and Victorian press, easels and shelves of other equipment. Everything in this room is meticulously ordered and arranged to be close to hand, exactly where it is needed. David's draughting table looks over a beautiful view of London rooftops.

LEFT Against one wall is a pinboard that David Gentleman uses to mock up layouts for his richly illustrated books. The tiny drawings here are a fragment of the spreads for his latest book, *London, You're Beautiful*, published in this Olympic year by Penguin Books. Gentleman produced a drawing of the city every day of the year, and takes us on a journey from (as we can see here) The British Museum, via Markets, Rivers, Lakes and Ponds, to East London and Richmond, Kew and Ham. The tiny pictures pinned in a grid to the wall allow Gentleman to arrange and rearrange each page of a book, and see everything in one go, until he is satisfied. Jars of brushes and pencils are arranged below.

BELOW In another corner of David Gentleman's studio, this collection of rulers and set squares reminds me of a composition by Ben Nicholson, with its balance of line and geometric shapes against a plain white background.

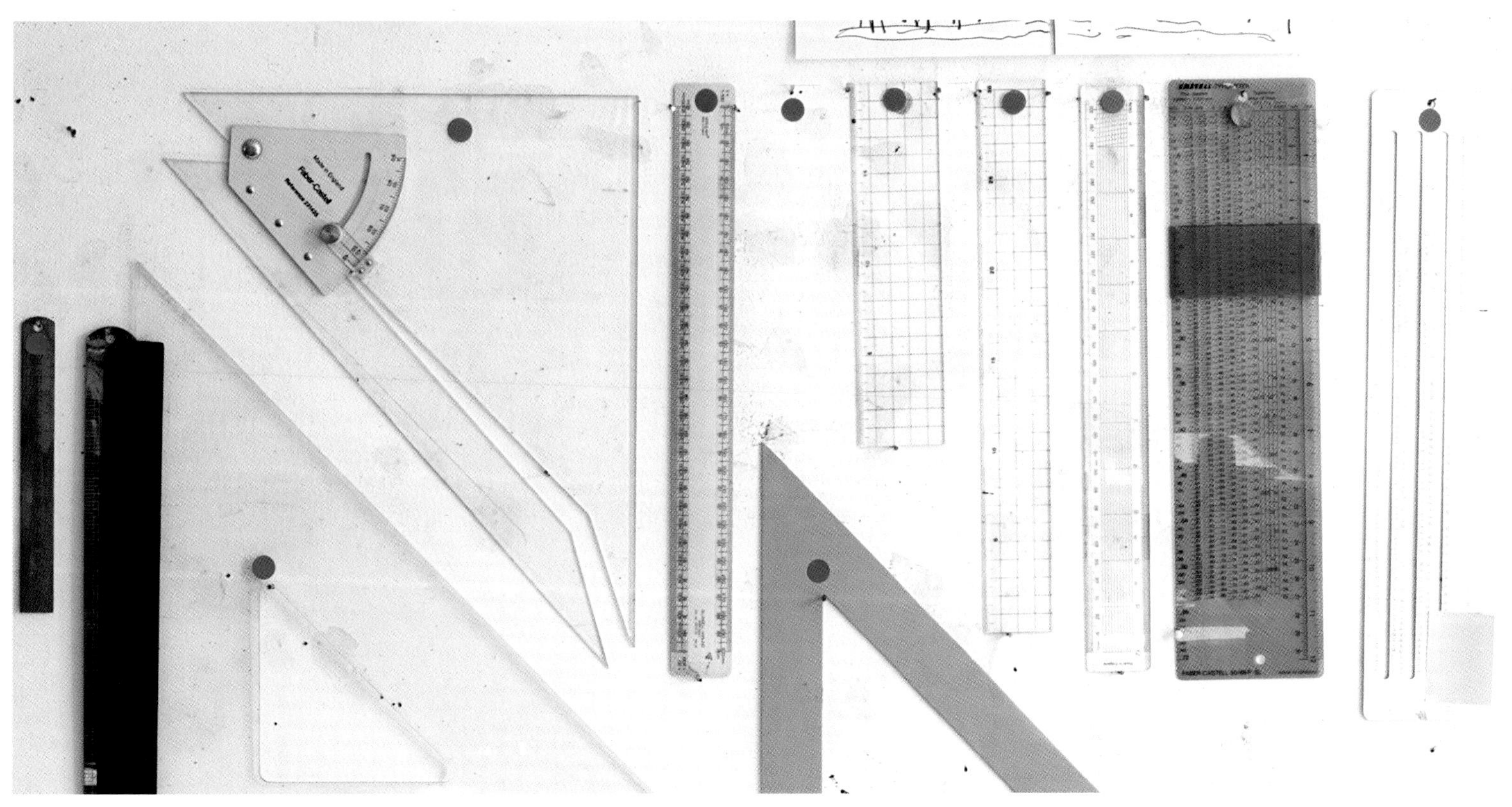

LEFT Bookbinder Charles Gledhill's studio on the top floor of his and Marianna Kennedy's house at Fournier Street, Spitalfields. Golden afternoon light streams into Charles's workshop, where the tools of his trade are arranged in carefully designed shelves and racks. Their appearance testifies to the unchanging nature of this ancient art: we could be in a bookbinding studio in seventeenth-century Paris or fifteenth-century Florence and not much would look different, save for the computer screen, radio, task lamps and cloth-wired lights with milk-glass shades. Rolls of bookcloth in rich colours await a new role in covering, protecting and announcing handsome books. Tools for gilding, and a press, are to the right. The walls are finished in plain beaded board.

BELOW A detail of the racks shows the hundreds of embossing wheels, mallets and punches used for making decorative gilded patterns on leather-bound covers and spines.

CHAPTER VII
Rooms of Display

WHAT TEMPLES OF RICHNESS are these? We English prefer, in general, a hearty but simple diet. We do not, as a rule, enjoy the consommés and pâtisserie of our continental neighbours, and this is as true of our rooms as our dinner plates. And yet, for high days and holidays, let us now feast, and enter the realm of the great collectors.

For centuries, the English have travelled and brought back home the dreams of foreign lands; transposed to our grey northern light. Just as we exported systems of government, transfer-printed tea sets and stiff upper lips around the world, so too did we voraciously bring the riches of other lands back home: Oriental china and Venetian glass, Indian textiles, Persian carpets, Italian and Greek architecture and antiquities.

Rich-coloured, many-layered, here we are in rooms of collectors for whom the space itself becomes part of the display. The cabinet of curiosities meets the land of naturalist–collectors and antiquarians; architects and magpies. There are peacocks lurking in each of us and, though we worry about the dust, and the cleaning, and the looking after, who can deny a quickened heart upon staring at the rooms now included? Like a trip to the theatre or to a glamorous restaurant—there is a time to banish modesty, to partake of the rich feast and to delight in the splendour of display.

I AM A COLLECTOR—I wonder if, deep down, we all are? My own passions, I sometimes think, are a little ubiquitous: Ravilious china, tulips and auriculas, mochaware jugs, books and more books on architecture and typography, and of engravings. In these passions I am not alone—a fact attested to not least by the recurrence of so many of these themes in the pages of this book.

I doubt I will ever stop the accumulation—a process that continues, and which you would notice (in subtle changes here and there) if you visited my rooms a mere six months from now—objects moved, rationalized, repositioned, and generally for a single purpose: to make room for more. One of the pleasures of owning a little shop in London is that when it is time for things to move on, there is a legitimate means by which they can do so. Of course, this merely becomes an excuse to collect more and more, without ever quite passing anything else on first. And then, of course, I find myself on bold new travels—since photographing this book, I have again gone mad, and dived this time into the glorious world of Fornasetti—but that is another story!

And so it is with many houses elsewhere in this book—that handsome kitchen dresser with its extraordinary collection of English delft; the remarkable study of a botanist in Suffolk; or the Scottish hall with its perfectly tempered blue and white china. But here, in each varied case, the collection is a part of a whole—contributory, but not the *raison d'etre*.

Poets and artists create dream spaces in which we can all dream and lose ourselves for a while, and these are the rooms we discover here in the final chapter of this book. These are the rooms that transcend the everyday, where their creator is working to a higher calling, making places that really can, for once, be described as unique.

So the great Peter Hone, whose remarkable, ever-expanding library of ornament bursts joyfully out of his Notting Hill flat, adds layer after layer and more. Plaster casts of leaves provide the latest diversion amongst the gods and goddesses of a previous incarnation.

Architect Craig Hamilton creates poetry in stone amongst the hills of Wales. Authentic and extraordinary, his drumbeat links directly to a song of two hundred years earlier, and his dream-making is the more remarkable for it; the gods really do draw near to the temple he is creating.

But Grand Tourists and dreamer–collectors (for these are our subject) come in curious shapes and guises. For, when scratching the surface a little deeper, what we also detect is that display is not merely the preserve of the grand and the classical. Low, comforting, manor-cottage interiors in far West Dorset, or a modernist lodge in Suffolk; David Gentlemen's carefully, beautifully tended catalogue of engraved wooded blocks—these can be part of the same dreamlike tendency; more subtle, more modest, but concerned with display for its own sake nonetheless.

I thrill to these rooms and moments as much as to their grander cousins. They are places that find their heart song in Goldfinger's Willow Road, amongst the collections of Conran or the vistas of Roche Court, or in the subtle, perfect world of Kettle's Yard. These are rooms and places that are, in their way, every bit as English as the grand country houses of past eras, and their owners take as much delight at the perfect proportions of a creamware cup, a leaf, a pebble or a feather as they do in more ordered art.

PAGE 158 AND PREVIOUS PAGES Vivid Pompeian colours and an exuberant Venetian glass chandelier transform an English dining room into a richly textured space. This extraordinary room is in the home of a distinguished classical architect and his wife. He designed the five columns that decorate the dining table; she stencilled and muralled the walls in intense, flaky distemper paint. Gilded Kent mirrors with Prince of Wales' feathers, Regency side tables with mirrored backs and a classical Italian painting in a rich gilt frame add to the dazzling sparkle on every surface. A pair of lions guards the fireplace; Persian bowls and lamps add a flash of cobalt blue and ultramarine. At night, by candlelight, this room is transformed into a glittering, historical place and we are, in an instant, transported away from the borders of Suffolk to eighteenth-century Italy.

RIGHT Artist David Gentleman has stored his wood engravings on a handsome set of shelves on the stair landing leading to his studio (illustrated on pages 154–155). This detail shot shows but several of the many hundreds of blocks, all painstakingly cut by hand in boxwood. Amongst his myriad talents, Gentleman is perhaps the most skilled engraver of his generation; the sharp-eyed will notice his logos for banks and insurance companies, as well as, at top left, the National Trust. Although entirely practical, these shelves create an absorbing display that one could look at for hours.

LEFT My great friend Peter Hone's mantelpiece at his astounding Notting Hill flat. No wall surface remains uncovered; every corner is filled with Peter's remarkable collection of classical architectural fragments, which must rank as one of the finest in the country and has earned these rooms the title 'The Hone Museum', so close a resemblance do they bear to the great nineteenth-century interiors created in Lincoln's Inn by the architect Sir John Soane. Happily, Peter reproduces many of his plaques and fragments in plaster, and we sell them in my shop. Either side of the white marble bust is a collection of Wedgwood creamware; the oak leaf pattern is a particular favourite of mine.

ABOVE AND OVERLEAF A corner of the same room is filled with urns and busts on plinths and pedestals. Peter designed and made the armchair, constructed from lion's paw feet and acanthus leaves. Everything happens at the broad, round table with its pink and white striped tablecloth. Overleaf, the full extent of Peter Hone's mania is revealed. These walls represent a lifetime's collecting; it is fascinating to see this flat in early copies of the *World of Interiors* from the 1980s, when just one or two key pieces are in place. This must act as a warning to all magpies and collectors, but, at the same time, gives us hope! Do not ask about the dusting.

Panasonic

ABOVE AND ABOVE LEFT The summer bedroom in Peter Hone's flat. Every corner is filled with fragments; around the Regency mirror hangs a huge collection, cast in oxblood, of historical figures that includes Shakespeare, Handel, Beethoven and Abraham Lincoln. The walls are painted eau-de-nil, a calm colour against which to display everything.

LEFT In the drawing room, casts of Ionic columns, classical busts and death masks lie alongside Peter's latest venture: casts of leaves gathered from the garden squares of Notting Hill, perfect in their chalky fragility.

RIGHT The collection bursts out into the hall of Peter Hone's flat; a classical panelled cupboard is subsumed under an advancing army of busts and statues. Peter, who used to run Clifton Nurseries in Little Venice, designed and makes the pier table in the foreground; the top can be formed either in plaster, stone or marble.

OVERLEAF This serene room is the creation of architect Craig Hamilton. Craig and his wife, the artist Diana Hulton, have transformed their Welsh farmhouse into a modern-day essay in the classical language. It is hard to believe that this is an entirely new building. Fragments from the Bassae Frieze line the walls, the ceiling is coffered and a pair of columns in turned wood are painted to simulate porphyry. The fireplace and much of the furniture were designed by Craig.

ABOVE In the entrance hallway of Craig Hamilton's house, works by the contemporary Scottish sculptor Alexander Stoddart sit alongside those by Schinkel, Thorvaldsen, and Christian Daniel Rauch. The ceiling is coffered and top-lit. The pale apricot walls are reminiscent of warmer Italian shores; solid stone steps lead down into the drawing room and library.

ABOVE RIGHT This tiny building, called 'The Athenian Treasury', was designed by Craig in 1999 to house his collection of architectural models and drawings. Craig is one of the finest architectural draughtsmen I know, and takes the time and care to record all his buildings with wooden models like those in the foreground, or in pencil or ink and wash presentation drawings. Here, they line the walls of this extraordinary jewel box; truly a room of display.

RIGHT AND FAR RIGHT Two views of Craig Hamilton's drawing office, in a converted barn at the farmhouse. The bust is of Gilly, the urns are nineteenth-century Italian terracotta from a limonaia, and architectural fragments and samples of mouldings and fine hardware rest on every surface (far right). Although the room is full, there is an underlying order to everything that is reminiscent of Craig's own buildings. Books fill the shelves; portraits of Craig Hamilton's heroes and his architectural drawings line the walls. The tiny cast-iron stove (right), with its delightful flue pipe, transports us to the world of nineteenth-century Sweden or Denmark.

English Brickwork

Ian Buruma
VOLTAIRE's coconuts
CONSIDERING CHILDREN
DAVID GRIBBLE
DK
THE HISTORY OF NORWAY
VOLPONE
M
EDWARD THOMAS · THERE WAS A TIME
HERBERT
PHOENIX
THE PILGRIM'S PROGRESS
Lucretius
COLLECTED POEMS OF W. B. YEATS
MACMILLAN AND CO
RUSSIAN THINKERS
ISAIAH BERLIN
THE OUTSIDER
SUMMER LIGHTNING
P. G. WODEHOUSE
THE AGE OF CAPITAL

Display need not be grand and does not require elaborate rooms with classical fragments. This is a corner of Jason and Kate Goodwin's little West Dorset manor house. The quiet display shows the brilliance with which Kate puts together her rooms; a disparate collection of lustreware, a china cockerel and surreal moulded-glass decanters sit alongside a child's drawing and a nineteenth-century playbill. I am obsessed with blackface letterpress typography; if I ever gave up architecture, I know I would have the happiest life as a printer, composing playbills and posters of this very nature. The text and fonts are mesmeric.

ABOVE The bathroom shelf of the house that we saw earlier on page 72. A collection of cobalt blue glassware—without which no English house is complete—is luminescent against the window. The pharmacy jar is a particularly nice example; although once common, they are now increasingly hard to find. Note the window glass, pressed with little sailing boats, reminiscent of the coastal location. In the foreground, a collection of mochaware and block colour mugs makes a useful spot for toothbrushes.

ABOVE RIGHT Birch-faced plywood stairs lead to the upstairs bedroom in this Suffolk house. Note the care with which the stairs are formed at the junction with the wall: simple materials, artfully used. Vivid yellow display cabinets, designed by the owner, house a collection of books, typographic memorabilia and other found objects, and pens and pencils just where they are needed. Cheeriest of all is the tomato red fish, a modern remake of an original pull-along on wobbly wheels designed by Alexander Calder.

RIGHT Another view of the same cabinets, which form a double-sided presentation niche at the same time as providing plenty of discreet, hidden storage. I love the fireworks of this bold yellow colour, in its own way as startling, and as happy, as the bright yellow entrance hall with which we opened this book. The owner is an inveterate collector; what we are seeing here is the tip of an iceberg. The shelves display a collection of early drinking glasses, jars from the old India Museum with handsome labels and boxes of antique glazed tile colour samples, bright with every colour of the rainbow.

ROWNTREE'S
2d
LIME CRISPS
ROWNTREE'S
LIME CRISPS

ARGYLL
ARGYLL

AFTERWORD

THIS BOOK HAS TAKEN US ON A JOURNEY: from houses humble to grand, from rooms unchanged for decades to others that are quite new. The ideas encompassed in each of them are unique. Yet I feel they belong to a coherent whole.

Even amongst the grand feast, there are moments of quiet relief; and even in the gentle rooms, there is a sense in each case of an eye, an artist, a designer, juxtaposing one thing with the next, combining, creating harmony—but always with an individual touch.

How, then, do we draw inspiration from these spaces? It may be as simple as learning new ways of using colour, or combining old furniture with new; looking at the way someone has arranged something, or designed a bookcase or dresser. But in a more general sense, these rooms offer us a mood. When looking at Jan Baldwin's remarkable photographs, I hope that you, like me, will have become absorbed and drawn in, so that you can taste, smell and hear the atmosphere as much as see it: the aromas in the kitchen, the stock pot on the stove; the sound of a ticking clock, or laughter just off camera.

It is these sounds and senses that make a home. How do we recognize spaces that are lived in, and loved? In part, it is through cherished possessions, each of which tells a story and carries a memory, from whom it came or where it was found. In part, it is through the care with which these rooms are put together, lovingly, over time. These are places that come alive with people—yet which have a spirit and character of their own. I do believe that houses can be sad, or happy, and can be brought to life with love and attention. There is something more to all this than mere bricks and mortar.

I am writing this on the very first day of the New Year, in Dorset: a time for reflection and anticipation. Great grey rainclouds are drenching the valley in layers of water and wind; black branches drip, and wintering plants are vivid and green against dark soil in the borders. The house is completely still. Yet even now, I am not alone. The flickering fire in the hearth; the slow ticking clock in the kitchen; the quiet, calm, gentle mass of this house, resting and present. If it is possible for a building to be a friend, solace and inspiration, then here, for me, it is. I trust this brief journey through this living world of English buildings and rooms has been as inspirational for you as it has been for me.

STYLE DIRECTORY

Decoration, furnishing fabrics and wallpapers

Adelphi wallpaper
00 1 518 284 9066
www.adelphipaperhangings.com
Beautifully printed papers.

Bennison
16 Holbein Place
London SW1W 8NL
+44 (0)20 7730 8076
www.bennisonfabrics.com
Classic faded English prints.

Chelsea Textiles
13 Walton Street
London SW3 2HX
+44 (0)20 7584 5544
www.chelseatextiles.com
For woven and hand-embroidered textiles.

Colefax and Fowler
39 Brook Street
London W1K 4JE
+44 (0)20 7493 2231
www.colefax.com
Still the grand old firm of English decoration, Colefax and Fowler's fabrics are unsurpassed.

De Gournay
112 Old Church Street
London SW3 6EP
+44 (0)20 7352 9988
www.degournay.com
Exquisite handpainted papers.

Hamilton Weston Wallpapers
Marryat Courtyard
88 Sheen Road
Richmond
Surrey TW9 1UF
+44 (0)20 8940 4850
www.hamiltonweston.com
Fine English papers and the home of Marthe Armitage, whose papers I adore.

Robert Kime
42–43 Museum Street
London WC1A 1LY
+44 (0)20 7831 6066
www.robertkime.com
Robert Kime is the greatest inspiration to me; the best fabrics, wallpapers and textiles alongside antique and perfectly reproduced lamps and furniture.

Ian Mankin
271/273 Wandsworth Bridge Road
London SW6 2TX
+44 (0)20 7722 0997
www.ianmankin.co.uk
I have always loved Ian Mankin's perfect tickings. No need to go anywhere else.

Jean Monro
Design Centre Chelsea Harbour
Lots Road
London SW10 0XE
+44 (0)20 7259 7281
www.jeanmonro.com
Simply the most beautiful English chintzes I know.

Svenskt Tenn
www.svenskttenn.se
available in the UK from:
Liberty
Regent Street
London W1B 5AH
+44 (0)20 7734 1234
www.liberty.co.uk
Wonderful Swedish textiles. I use many Josef Frank fabrics at home.

Furniture

The Conran Shop
Michelin House
81 Fulham Road
London SW3 6RD
+44 (0)20 7589 7401
www.conranshop.co.uk
Some of the finest contemporary furniture and accessories.

Howard Chairs Ltd
30–31 Lyme Street
London NW1 0EE
+44 (0)20 7482 2156
www.howardchairs.freeserve.co.uk
The best English chairs and sofas, from a 200-year-old company.

Howe
93 Pimlico Road
London SW1W 8PH
+44 (0)20 7730 7987
www.howelondon.com
I love the brilliant displays and perfect combinations of new and old at Christopher Howe's showroom.

Edward Hurst
The Battery
Rockbourne Road
Coombe Bissett
Salisbury
Wiltshire SP5 4LP
+44 (0)1722 718859
www.edwardhurst.com
Edward Hurst is one of the finest dealers of his generation.

Max Rollitt
The Old Telephone Exchange
Station Road
Alresford
Hampshire SO24 9JG
+44 (0)1962 738800
www.maxrollit.com
My great friend Max has one of the keenest eyes for antiques, and makes perfect reproductions.

George Sherlock
3 Hornet Close
Broadstairs
Kent CT10 2YD
+44 (0)1843 864190
www.georgesherlock.com
Classic English sofas in trademark pink calico at surprisingly affordable prices.

Westenholz Antiques
80–82 Pimlico Road
London SW1 8PL
+44 (0)20 7824 8090
www.westenholz.co.uk
The perfect combination of decorative and robust in antique furniture and lighting

Lighting

The English House
+44 (0)1502 478493
www.theenglishhouse.co.uk
Charles Morris's beautiful handmade steel fixtures are at home in a traditional or contemporary setting.

Jamb
107A Pimlico Road
London SW1W 8PH
+ 44 (0)20 7730 2122
www.jamblimited.com
Will Fisher's reproduction lights are as beautiful and perfectly made as his range of reproduction fire surrounds.

Marianna Kennedy
www.mariannakennedy.com
Marianna's resin lights feature in many pages of this book. Brilliant at enlivening an otherwise quiet space.

Soane
50–52 Pimlico Road
London, SW1W 8LP
+44 (0)20 7730 6400
www.soane.co.uk
Reproduction lighting, handsome furniture and interesting textiles.

Rugs and Flooring

Malabar Trading
33 South Street,
Bridport
Dorset DT6 3NY
+44 (0)1308 425734
www.malabartrading.com
Robyn Huxter is one of my secret sources for excellent rugs and kelims.

The Alternative Flooring Company
www.alternativeflooring.com
My favourite source for natural floorcoverings, which I much prefer to fitted wool carpets.

Hardware and Bathroom

Aston Matthews
141/147a Essex Road
London N1 2SN
+ 44 (0)20 7226 7220
www.astonmatthews.co.uk
A very reliable source for bathroom fixtures and fittings.

Holloways of Ludlow
121 Shepherd's Bush Road
London W6 7LP
+ 44 (0)20 7602 5757
www.hollowaysofludlow.com
An excellent source of architectural hardware and interior and exterior lighting, at reasonable prices.

Optimum Brasses
+44 (0)1398 331515
www.optimumbrasses.com
Excellent reproduction hardware.

Paint

Farrow & Ball
www.farrow-ball.com
Needs no introduction: some of the finest English paints available. Hold onto old colour charts for dear life, to be able to specify discontinued colours.

Paint & Paper Library
5 Elystan Street
London SW3 3NT
+44 (0)20 7590 9860
www.paintlibrary.co.uk
David Oliver's inspired selection of colours.

Papers and Paints
4 Park Walk
London SW10 0AD
+ 44 (0)20 7352 8626
www.papers-paints.co.uk
A brilliant range of beautifully made paint.

Auctions

I always head for a local country auction house whenever I see it. My favourite local auction in London is Criterion, based in Islington and Wandsworth:
www.criterionauctioneers.com

Pictures

Abbott and Holder
30 Museum Street
London, WC1A 1LH
+ 44 (0)20 7637 3981
www.abbottandholder-thelist.co.uk
To my mind, the friendliest and best-value dealer in London.

For absolutely everything

Ben Pentreath Ltd.
17 Rugby Street
WC1N 3QT
+ 44 (0)20 7430 2526
My own little shop in London's Bloomsbury.

SWEET TREATS
Lemon Cream
Meringues
Grape Jelly
Chocolate Cream
Trifle
Stewed Pears
CHEESE
990
3

BUCKINGHAMSHIRE
CAMBRIDGESHIRE
CHESHIRE
CORNWALL
CUMBRIA
DERBYSHIRE
DEVON
DORSET
COUNTY DURHAM
ESSEX
GLOUCESTERSHIRE 1: THE COTSWOLDS
GLOUCESTERSHIRE 2: THE VALE AND THE FOREST OF DEAN
HAMPSHIRE: WINCHESTER AND THE NORTH
HEREFORDSHIRE
HERTFORDSHIRE
ISLE OF WIGHT
NORTH EAST AND EAST KENT
WEST KENT AND THE WEALD
LANCASHIRE: NORTH
LANCASHIRE: LIVERPOOL AND THE SOUTH-WEST
LANCASHIRE: MANCHESTER AND THE SOUTH-EAST
LEICESTERSHIRE AND RUTLAND
LONDON 6: WESTMINSTER
NORFOLK 1: NORWICH AND NORTH-EAST
NORFOLK 2: NORTH-WEST AND SOUTH
NORTHAMPTONSHIRE
NORTHUMBERLAND
NOTTINGHAMSHIRE
OXFORDSHIRE
SHROPSHIRE
STAFFORDSHIRE
SUFFOLK
England
SURREY
WARWICKSHIRE
WORCESTERSHIRE
YORKSHIRE: YORK AND THE EAST RIDING
YORKSHIRE WEST RIDING
THE CATHEDRALS OF ENGLAND
FIFE
GWYNEDD
HIGHLAND AND ISLANDS
PERTH AND KINROSS
STIRLING AND CENTRAL SCOTLAND
CARMARTHENSHIRE AND CEREDIGION
CLWYD
GLAMORGAN
GWENT/MONMOUTHSHIRE
PEMBROKESHIRE
POWYS
DUBLIN
NORTH LEINSTER
NORTH WEST ULSTER
Inigo Jones
JAMES LEES-MILNE
Hawksmoor
Dictionary & Usage
The Concise Oxford Dictionary
Illustrated Glossary of Architecture
ARCHITECTURE IN BRITAIN & IRELAND
PHOTOSHOP CS3 in easy steps
LIFE WITH THE LOCALS by HENRY BENHAM
iMac
Mac OS X Illustrated
THE GRACES
JOHN NASH
PUGIN
Victorian Architecture
BLOMFIELD
GOTHIC
THE ENGLISH
GREAT INTERIORS
Preface by
SCRUTON
The Classical Vernacular
10 DOWNING STREET
OXFORD ORIGINALS
Classical America IV
ARCHITECTS ANONYMOUS
The Regional Books
BRECKLAND
Olive Cook
THE FUNCTIONAL TRADITION
J. M. Richards
Designs for 20th-century Interiors
VICTORIAN
THE ENGLISHMAN'S ROOM
The World of Mary Ellen Best
DECORATION
APOLLO JULY 1977

BOOKSHELF

Although this is not an exhaustive list, these are some of the books on my own shelves to which I return time and again. They are ideal for providing further inspiration, where it is needed.

Vanessa Berridge (editor), *The English Country Home*, London 1987

Ros Byam Shaw, *Old House New Home*, London 2005

Mirabel Cecil and David Mlinaric, *Mlinaric on Decorating*, London 2008

Stafford Cliff and Gilles de Chabaneix, *The Way We Live*, London 2003

Terence Conran, *The House Book*, London 1974

Terence Conran and Stafford Cliff, *Terence Conran's Inspiration: At Home with Design*, London 2008

John Cornforth, *English Interiors 1790–1848: The Quest for Comfort*, London 1978

Estelle Ellis and Caroline Seebohm, *At Home with Books*, New York 1995

John Fowler and John Cornforth, *English Decoration in the 18th Century*, London 1974

Joseph Friedman, *Paint and Colour in Decoration*, London 2003

The Knight of Glin and James Peill, *Irish Furniture*, New Haven and London 2007

The Knight of Glin & James Peill, *The Irish Country House*, London 2010

Alan and Ann Gore, *The History of English Interiors*, London 1991

Sally Griffiths and Simon McBride, *The English House: Architecture and Interiors*, London 2004

Ashley Hicks, *David Hicks: A Life of Design*, New York 2009

David Hicks, *David Hicks on Decoration, London*, London 1966

David Hicks, *David Hicks on Living – With Taste*, London 1968

David Hicks, *David Hicks on Decoration – With Fabrics*, London 1971

David Hicks, *David Hicks on Decoration – 5*, London 1972

David Hicks, *Living with Design*, London 1979

Min Hogg and Wendy Harrop, *The World of Interiors: A Decoration Book*, London 1988

Horst, *Vogue's Book of Houses, Gardens, People*, London 1968

Chippy Irvine and Christopher Simon Sykes, *The English Room*, London 2001

Gervase Jackson-Stops and James Pipkin, *The English Country House: A Grand Tour*, London 1984

Chester Jones, *Colefax & Fowler: The Best in English Interior Decoration*, London 1989

Alvilde Lees-Milne and Derry Moore, *The Englishwoman's House*, London 1984

Alvilde Lees-Milne and Derry Moore, *The Englishman's Room*, Harmondsworth 1986

Mary Miers, *The English Country House*, New York 2009

Derry Moore and Michael Pick, *The English Room*, London 1985

Jeremy Musson, *English Country House Interiors*, New York 2011

Walter Pfeiffer and Marianne Heron, *In the Houses of Ireland*, New York 1988

Paige Rense (editor), *Architectural Digest: International Interiors*, Los Angeles 1979

Suzanne Slesin and Stafford Cliff, *English Style*, New York 1984

Henrietta Spencer-Churchill, *Classic Georgian Style*, London 1997

Peter Ward-Jackson, *English Furniture Designs of the Eighteenth Century*, London 1958

Martin Wood, *John Fowler, Prince of Decorators*, London 2007

BUSINESS CREDITS

Architects and designers whose work is featured in this book:

Ruth Guilding
www.bibleofbritishtaste.com
Pages 8; 53; 58–61; 95; 141.

Craig Hamilton Architects Ltd
+44 (0)1982 570491
admin@craighamiltonarchitects.com
www.craighamiltonarchitects.com
and
Diana Hulton
Diana@dianahulton.com
www.dianahulton.com
Pages 151 left; 76–77; 102–103; 170–173.

Peter Hone
Peter Hone's work is available at
Ben Pentreath Ltd
17 Rugby Street
London WC1N 3QT
+44 (0)20 7430 2526
For other commissions, please contact Peter Hone on +44 (0)20 7221 5872
Pages 25 above right; 88; 164–169.

Marianna Kennedy
Artist/Designer
and
James Howett (works with Marianna)
+44 (0)20 7375 2787
mkennedy@mariannakennedy.com
www.mariannakennedy.com
Pages 42 below left; 66–67; 98–99; 121; 134; 156–157.

Arne Maynard
www.arnemaynard.com
Pages 72 above right; 73; 104–105; 124–125; 132–133; 147 above right; 149 above; 190–191.

Ben Pentreath Ltd
17 Rugby Street
Bloomsbury
London WC1N 3QT
+44 (0)20 7430 2526
shop@benpentreath.com

Interior decoration projects:
interiors@benpentreath.com

Architecture projects:
architecture@benpentreath.com
Pages 1; 3; 10; 15; 25 below left; 54–57; 68–69; 83–85; 90; 97; 106–109; 122–123; 130 above right; 183; 192.

Pocknell Studio
+44 (0)1371 850075
dp@pocknellstudio.com
www.pocknellstudio.com
and
Webb & Webb Design Limited
design@webbandwebb.co.uk
www.webbandwebb.co.uk

George Saumarez Smith
ADAM Architecture
Old Hyde House
Winchester SO23 7DW
+44 (0)1962 843843
georgess@adamarchitecture.com
www.adamarchitecture.com
Pages 42 above left; 70–71; 100–101; 118–119

Quinlan & Francis Terry LLP
Old Exchange
High Street
Dedham
Colchester CO7 6HA
+44 (0)1206 323186
email@qftarchitects.com
www.qftarchitects.com
Pages 43; 144 above; 150; 158–161.

PICTURE CREDITS

All photography by Jan Baldwin, except where otherwise stated.

Every effort has been made to trace the copyright holders, architects and designers. We apologize in advance for any unintentional omissions and would be pleased to insert the appropriate acknowledgement in any subsequent edition.

1 Ben Pentreath's London flat; 2 Caddy and Chris Wilmot-Sitwell's house in Dorset; 3 Ben Pentreath's Dorset house; 6–7 Kate and Jason Goodwin's house in Dorset; 8 Ruth Guilding and A. N.Wilson's London house; 10 Ben Pentreath's London flat; 15 Ben Pentreath's London flat; 18 © Estate of Horst P. Horst/Art + Commerce; 21 © Fritz von der Schulenburg/The Interior Archive; 22 © Ken Kirkwood photographer; 25 above left Garsington Manor, home of Mrs Rosalind Ingrams and her family; 25 above right Peter Hone's home in London; 25 below left Ben Pentreath's London flat; 25 below right Caddy and Chris Wilmot-Sitwell's house in Dorset; 29 The East Front of Kelmscott Manor, frontispiece of News from Nowhere by William Morris, engraved by W.H. Hooper, 1892 (woodcut) by Gere, Charles March (1869-1957) (after); Private Collection/The Bridgeman Art Library; Nationality/copyright status: English/in copyright until 2028; 33–35 Caddy and Chris Wilmot-Sitwell's house in Dorset; 36–37 The home of Iain and Zara Milligan in Scotland; 40–41 Garsington Manor, home of Mrs Rosalind Ingrams and her family; 42 above left George Saumarez Smith's home in Winchester; 42 above right Sue and David Gentleman's house in London; 42 below left Marianna Kennedy, 3 Fournier Street, Spitalfields; 43 Higham Hall, family home of Quinlan and Christine Terry; 44–45 Anon; 46–47 The home of Iain and Zara Milligan in Scotland; 48–51 Garsington Manor, home of Mrs Rosalind Ingrams and her family; 53 Ruth Guilding and A. N.Wilson's London house; 54–57 Ben Pentreath's Dorset house; 58–61 Ruth Guilding and A. N.Wilson's London house; 66–67 Marianna Kennedy, 3 Fournier Street, Spitalfields; 68–69 Ben Pentreath's London flat; 70–71 George Saumarez Smith's home in Winchester; 72 above right and 73 Garden Designer Arne Maynard and William Collinson's home in Monmouthshire; 74–75 Kate and Jason Goodwin's house in Dorset; 76–77 Architect Craig Hamilton and artist Diana Hulton's home in Wales; 83–85 Ben Pentreath's Dorset house; 86–87 The home of Iain and Zara Milligan in Scotland; 88 Peter Hone's home in London; 89 Garsington Manor, home of Mrs Rosalind Ingrams and her family; 90 Ben Pentreath's Dorset house; 92–94 Sue and David Gentleman's house in London; 95 Ruth Guilding and A. N.Wilson's London house; 96–97 Ben Pentreath's London flat; 98–99 Marianna Kennedy, 3 Fournier Street, Spitalfields; 100–101 George Saumarez Smith's home in Winchester; 102–103 Architect Craig Hamilton and artist Diana Hulton's home in Wales; 104–105 Garden designer Arne Maynard and William Collinson's home in Monmouthshire; 106–109 Ben Pentreath's Dorset house; 112–113 The home of Iain and Zara Milligan in Scotland; 114–115 Garsington Manor, home of Mrs Rosalind Ingrams and her family; 117 Garsington Manor, home of Mrs Rosalind Ingrams and her family; 118–119 George Saumarez Smith's home in Winchester; 120 Sue and David Gentleman's house in London; 121 Marianna Kennedy, 3 Fournier Street, Spitalfields; 122–123 Ben Pentreath's Dorset house; 124–125 Garden designer Arne Maynard and William Collinson's home in Monmouthshire; 126–127 Sue and David Gentleman's house in Suffolk; 130 above and below left The home of Iain and Zara Milligan in Scotland; 130 above right Ben Pentreath's Dorset house; 131 Ben Pentreath's Dorset house; 132–133 Garden designer Arne Maynard and William Collinson's home in Monmouthshire; 134 Marianna Kennedy, 3 Fournier Street, Spitalfields; 136–139 Garsington Manor, home of Mrs Rosalind Ingrams and her family; 141 Ruth Guilding and A. N.Wilson's London house; 142 Sue and David Gentleman's house in Suffolk; 143 Garsington Manor, home of Mrs Rosalind Ingrams and her family; 144 above Higham Hall, family home of Quinlan and Christine Terry; 144 below The home of Iain and Zara Milligan in Scotland; 145 Garsington Manor, home of Mrs Rosalind Ingrams and her family; 147 above right Garden designer Arne Maynard and William Collinson's home in Monmouthshire; 147 below The home of Iain and Zara Milligan in Scotland; 149 above Garden designer Arne Maynard and William Collinson's home in Monmouthshire; 149 below Sue and David Gentleman's house in Suffolk; 150 Higham Hall, family home of Quinlan and Christine Terry; 151 left Architect Craig Hamilton and artist Diana Hulton's home in Wales; 151 right Garsington Manor, home of Mrs Rosalind Ingrams and her family; 152–155 Sue and David Gentleman's house in Suffolk; 156–157 Marianna Kennedy, 3 Fournier Street, Spitalfields; 158–161 Higham Hall, family home of Quinlan and Christine Terry; 163 Sue and David Gentleman's house in London; 164–169 Peter Hone's home in London; 170–173 Architect Craig Hamilton and artist Diana Hulton's home in Wales; 174–175 Kate and Jason Goodwin's house in Dorset; 183 Ben Pentreath's London shop; 190–191 Garden designer Arne Maynard and William Collinson's home in Monmouthshire; 192 Ben Pentreath's London shop.

The Dictionary of
National
Biography
1971-1980
Oxford

INDEX

Figures in italics indicate captions.

ACKNOWLEDGMENTS

I am greatly indebted to my many friends who allowed Jan and me to visit their houses and photograph their rooms for this book. Without them, and their generous welcome, it would not have taken shape. Many happy lunches were eaten in these lovely rooms!

I am particularly grateful to all at Ryland Peters & Small for their assistance; and especially to Alison Starling, who first approached me about writing a book on this subject. Cindy Richards, Leslie Harrington, Toni Kay and Annabel Morgan looked after me every step of the way, and Emily Westlake contributed a quiet sense of organization to the complicated process of fixing the logistics.

I am very grateful to Nicky Haslam for the generous introduction, and for Ruth Guilding's help in arranging this.

Jan Baldwin was more fun to work with than I could have imagined. She has a brilliant eye, was tolerant of my interference and remained completely calm at all times (even having collapsed my dining table when laden with crockery and glass). The photographs in this book are testament to her skill.

My mother read the final manuscript, William Smalley and George Saumarez Smith both helped me work out what I was thinking when I had forgotten, and Valentina Rice kept me excited about the book the whole time.